Lord Durham's *Report on the Affairs of British North America* is usually discussed only in terms of its historical context – the events that brought Durham to Canada and the consequences of the Report's reform proposals. In a markedly different approach, Janet Ajzenstat treats the Report as a text in modern political thought. She develops Durham's underlying arguments and assumptions, demonstrating the essentially liberal character of his recommendations and revealing a tough-minded argument about political freedom and the place of national minorities in a free society.

While the standard interpretation has portrayed Durham as prejudiced and ignorant about French Canada, Ajzenstat shows that, on the contrary, the assimilation proposal follows from Durham's consideration of ways of opening the widest political and economic opportunities for French Canadians. She argues that far from being "racist," as so many historians have suggested, Durham's proposals reflect the tolerance at the heart of liberalism that prohibits discrimination on the basis of race, origin, or creed.

Ajzenstat suggests that Durham's argument clarifies what she sees as a present dilemma for Canada: that legislation intended to protect cherished minority traditions necessarily erodes liberal rights that those minorities hold equally dear.

The Political Thought of Lord Durham provides a new direction for our understanding of liberalism. It will be of interest to everyone concerned with issues of justice, freedom, and nationality.

Janet Ajzenstat teaches in the Department of Political Science, McMaster University.

The Political Thought

of Lord Durham

JANET AJZENSTAT

McGill-Queen's University Press
Kingston and Montreal

© McGill-Queen's University Press 1988
ISBN 0-7735-0637-3

Legal deposit 1st quarter 1988
Bibliothèque nationale du Québec

Printed in Canada

This book has been published with the help of a grant from
the Social Science Federation of Canada, using funds
provided by the Social Sciences and Humanities Research
Council of Canada.

∞

Printed on acid-free paper

Canadian Cataloguing in Publication Data

Ajzenstat, Janet, 1936-
  The political thought of Lord Durham
  Includes bibliographical references and index.
  ISBN 0-7735-0637-3
  1. Durham, John George Lambton, Earl of, 1792-1840 —
  Political and social views. 2. Durham, John George Lambton,
  Earl of, 1792-1840. Report on the affairs of British North America.
  3. Canada — History — 1791-1841. 4. Canada — Politics and
  government — 1838-1841. I. Title.
  FC462.A44 1987 971.03'9 C87-090244-X
  F1032.A44 1987

To Florence Gibson MacDonald

Contents

Preface

This is a book about one man's thought on liberal justice and nationalism, freedom and democracy. Its aim is modest in one sense. I describe one thinker and concentrate on one text. But in another sense it could be called ambitious because I try to show how that thinker tackles questions of timeless interest.

I treat the Durham Report as a text in modern political philosophy. I have looked for a general political teaching in Durham's analysis of the Canadian crisis of the 1830s. I hope, of course, that my exposition will interest those who want a fuller picture of the Durham mission, but it is meant first of all for readers concerned with the issues of freedom and justice today. Because the teaching in the Report is given in terms of an analysis of the events of the time, I have had to consider those events, as historians also do. Nevertheless my concern is not primarily to describe the facts or even to give Durham's view of them; it is rather to develop an understanding of the theoretical assumptions and arguments informing his observations.

My approach may be unfamiliar to historians, but will be easily recognized by those students of political philosophy who commonly turn to texts like *The Federalist Papers*, or Tocqueville's *Democracy in America*, for insights into the politics of our day. I am not suggesting that these students believe that Madison's constitutional proposals or Tocqueville's observations of the United States in 1832 relate in all detail to the politics of our time. The argument is rather that from these writers' reflections on the problems of their period, we can derive – as they themselves intended – a general understanding of political matters, and that this in turn can facilitate thought about the politics of many periods, including ours.

For Durham, faced in 1838 with the "fatal feud" between the French- and English-speaking colonists in Lower Canada, and the profound dissatisfaction with British policies prevailing in all the colonies, the more general problem was to persuade both his French and English readers (and the home-country imperialists as well as the colonial radicals) that insofar as they valued liberal justice, equality of opportunity, and political freedom, their grievances could be met by making colonial institutions more like the British. In short, the Report was written to defend the British constitution and the institutions of British liberalism. It is not couched in abstract language, and does not have the form of a theoretical treatise. Nevertheless, I believe that the author meant each example, argument, and proposal to point to a coherent teaching about the best possible form of government.

I have not attempted to place this teaching in a broad historical context. While I discuss the articles and documents pertaining to Canada that Durham read in the months before the Canadian mission, in the main my focus is narrow. Some readers may be uneasy because I do so little to show Durham in relation to earlier and later periods. But I would argue that the attempt to place him in this way, where the assumption may be that earlier ideas are necessarily superseded by later (and that the later are superior), is not essential to describing or assessing him, and may indeed militate against seeing him clearly. Often enough, talk of seeing historical figures in the context of their age simply masks the fact that the writer is bringing twentieth-century prejudices to bear. So Durham is often described as a "racist." But this point of view, as I shall show, depends on the curiously arrogant assumption that the men of the past were blinkered as we are not. Gerald Craig suggests, for example, that "Lord Durham could not know as clearly in 1838 what we know today."[1] Ged Martin argues that we cannot measure Durham by twentieth-century standards.[2] Their position surely shows little respect for Durham's standards. A very different picture emerges, as we shall see, when we approach the Report with the assumption that it may contain coherent and relevant ideas.

What I argue in the chapters that follow depends on the idea that from at least the beginnings of the modern period – from 1688, if we think in terms of practical politics in Britain – there has been an ongoing debate about certain issues, chiefly the practical consequences of the principles of tolerance and equality – and that although it is sometimes possible to trace a sequence of ideas, and show how one thinker influenced another, there is no reason to suppose that earlier arguments must be less illuminating simply because they are earlier. In the seventeenth century this ongoing debate turned on Hobbes's argument that all men must be regarded as equal. So Locke maintains in *The Letter Concerning Toleration* that the intolerant are not to be tolerated, and by the "intolerant" he means those who will not acknowledge the equality of men in the "outward court," to use his term, that is, in the political arena, but instead insist on the superiority of individuals or political factions claiming the sanction of God, conscience, nature.[3] With the Glorious Revolution and the Toleration Act of 1689, England adopted Locke's argument, abandoning the public, political use of religious beliefs. After the revolution, no party or faction was to compete as agent of God's will; no authority in politics was to be based on uncompromising beliefs and principles transcending the *salus populi* and popular consent.

For later figures, like Durham, the debate on tolerance takes another form. But it is recognizably the same debate, and still depends on Hobbes's equality principle. In Locke's time what was feared was tyrannical government by divine-right kings, or priestly hierarchies. By Durham's day it was clear that those who advanced uncompromising demands in the name of "race" or national origin were as intolerant as any priestly faction. True, an uncompromising minority nationality was unlikely to be a threat to the liberty of the majority in the way that kings or hierarchies were a threat. Such a minority was more probably the object of exploitation. Nevertheless, the same principles applied: laws protecting an exploited intolerant minority were no more to be tolerated in a liberal society than laws protecting a ruling intolerant tyrant.

I develop this argument in the chapters to follow and show how Durham belongs in the camp of tolerance, not racism. Here I wish only to suggest that my approach to the Report, ahistorical as it may seem, will give us a truer picture of Durham than Craig's and Martin's attempt at objectivity because it is open to the central issue with which Durham was concerned. Indeed, since the debate on matters of tolerance is crucial to liberalism in all periods, including Durham's, I would even say that I give a truer picture of him in relation to his own time.

As the mention of Madison and Tocqueville above suggests, the practice of studying historical documents for political insights is perhaps more common in the United States than in Canada. But there is no reason to suppose that the British and Canadians concerned with the government of British North America were any less shrewd and well educated than the Americans, or that the problems of the northern colonies are less interesting theoretically. From my own experience of the material I am convinced that, on the contrary, Canadian documentary history contains an almost unrivaled commentary on the modern debate about tolerance.

It has been said that North America is the proving ground for the political thought of Hobbes and Locke.[4] In a society where the grip of old customs was looser, the full consequences of Hobbes's equality principle first came to light. It is true that we are as apt to find arguments about equality and freedom in American documents as Canadian. Part of the interest of the Canadian material lies in seeing those arguments worked out in terms of British parliamentary institutions. But the great importance of Canadian historical documents, I believe, has to do with the fact that this country exhibited the problem of nationality as the United States did not. There was no social cleavage in the United States comparable to that of the "two nations" in British North America. In the case of Lower Canada, observers had to consider equality and nationality together. The Canadian situation forced observers to reflect on that problem of equality and tolerance in ways that the American did not.

The Durham Report is only one example. I would argue that it was the confrontation of French and English in Canada that brought thinkers in the liberal tradition to see how the claims of nationalist groups would violate Hobbes's principle.[5]

The fact is that there is no argument in the philosophy of Hobbes and Locke by which the English – as English, as a collectivity – could assert title to rule. True, the equality principle was often ignored as the business of empire went on and rule by the English was promoted in one fashion or another. Durham rages against the imperial government's habit of opening political opportunities to the English and denying them to the French. Nevertheless, it remained true that by liberal principles the conquered were as entitled to participate in government as the conquerors. From 1760 the point was made by both French and English that if there was to be a legislative assembly or governing council in Quebec, the French were justified in demanding seats on the same basis as the English. All in all a remarkable number of Canadian documents take up this and related questions. For how were men differing in origin, language, religion, and political education to learn to govern in concert?

To refuse to make those earlier observers a party to the debate as we know it today is to lose the opportunity to consider insights they had and we may have forgotten, or – even where we judge them wrong – to illuminate the ground of our own thought by trying to understand theirs. Durham was not a philosopher. He did not question the political doctrine he espoused or debate its assumptions. But he knew the perennial issues of the modern liberal tradition, and he was thoroughly familiar with the theory and practices of British liberalism. In the *Report on the Affairs of British North America* there is a comprehensive statement about the conditions for political freedom and the place of nationalities in a liberal society that can still inform and may still convince.

Acknowledgments

I should like to think that this book does justice to two of my teachers, Peter Russell and Allan Bloom. Professor Russell supervised my doctoral dissertation on Lord Durham at the University of Toronto. I am fortunate indeed if *The Political Thought of Lord Durham* reflects something of his balanced understanding of politics. To Professor Bloom I owe the suggestion that I undertake the study of Canadian historical documents from the perspective of a student of political philosophy. I shall always be grateful for this counsel, and for the avenues of thought opened by his lectures at the University of Toronto.

Many friends and teachers helped during those graduate years at Toronto. I must mention especially Professor Robert A. Fenn, who taught me to give enough attention to the historical context, and how to know what "enough" attention is, and Professor Donald Smiley, who was always strict and always encouraging.

I owe a debt to too many at McMaster University to name them all. McMaster has been home base in recent years, sometimes an employer, sometimes an "accommodation address." I should like to thank Harry Turner for his comments on what has become chapter seven, Howard Brotz for many thought-provoking discussions about nationality, and John Seaman (who read the whole of an earlier draft) for his most helpful criticisms about the organization of the material. My thanks go as well to the librarians at Mills Memorial Library for their courtesy, and courtesy cards.

I am grateful, too, for the comments of professors Reginald Whitaker, Daniel Latouche, and Reader "B" on the final manuscript. I have no doubt that discussion about the matters they raise will continue. To Lydia Burton, I owe thanks for the tact and skill she brought to the task of editing.

I am very glad to acknowledge the assistance of the Social Sciences and Humanities Research Council of Canada. This help, in the form of a postdoctoral fellowship and a research grant came at a time, 1980 to 1982, when

I might well have given up academic studies. *The Political Thought of Lord Durham* has been published with the help of a grant from the Social Science Federation of Canada, using funds provided by the Social Sciences and Humanities Research Council of Canada.

I acknowledge with thanks permission to use material previously published in several forms: material in chapter two originally appeared in "Liberalism and Assimilation: Lord Durham Reconsidered," in Stephen Brooks's *Political Thought in Canada* (Irwin Publishing 1984). Arguments in chapters six and seven are adapted from "Modern Mixed Government: A Liberal Defence of Inequality," *Canadian Journal of Political Science* (March 1985), and "Liberalism and Nationality," *Canadian Journal of Political Science* (September 1981). The material on Roebuck first appeared in "Collectivity and Individual Right in 'Mainstream' Liberalism: John Arthur Roebuck and the *Patriotes*," *Journal of Canadian Studies* (September 1984); and the themes in chapter eight were first explored in "French Canada and the Liberal Theory of Nationality: Some Now Unpopular 19th Century Ideas," in the *Dalhousie Review* (Summer 1985).

All my ideas have been developed through discussions with Samuel Ajzenstat – discussions that are at once the greatest help, and the greatest pleasure.

The Political Thought of Lord Durham

CHAPTER ONE

Durham's Liberalism

"There are two modes by which a government may deal with a conquered territory," argues Lord Durham in the *Report on the Affairs of British North America*. The first requires the conquerors to respect "the rights and nationality of the actual occupants." The second, he goes on, "is that of treating the conquered territory as one open to the conquerors, of encouraging their influx, of regarding the conquered race as entirely subordinate, and of endeavouring as speedily and as rapidly as possible to assimilate the character and institutions of its new subjects to those of the great body of its empire."[1]

Durham maintained that the scale of British immigration to Lower Canada had made it impossible for the British government to adopt the first "mode" in 1838. He was convinced that the assimilation of the French Canadians "as speedily as possible" was the only feasible course left, and to bring assimilation about he recommended that the imperial parliament pass a bill uniting the two Canadian provinces. The supposition was that the French-speaking people of the lower province would forever abandon their "vain endeavour to preserve a French Canadian nationality," once they were subjected to the "vigorous rule of an English majority."[2]

"I entertain no doubts as to the national character which must be given to Lower Canada," he writes; "it must be that of the British Empire; that of the majority of the population of British America; that of the great race which must, in the lapse of no long period of time, be predominant over the whole North American Continent."[3]

That the French in Canada must assimilate is nothing less than the central tenet of the Report. In Durham's view all hope of peace in the colonies and all prospects for political reform hung on the assimilation proposal. He argued that other observers of the time had made the mistake of supposing that political reforms alone would remedy the ills of British North America, and that his prescription was superior precisely because he had seen that there was a "far deeper and far more efficient cause – a cause which penetrated beneath [Lower Canada's] political institutions into its social state."[4] And that cause, he maintained, was the "fatal feud of origin," the struggle between French and English.

Almost without exception Durham's commentators have found this argument offensive. As William Ormsby puts it in his essay, "Lord Durham and the Assimilation of French Canada," the Report taken as a whole is usually said to be "perceptive and significant," but the assimilation proposal is "deplored as indicative of a regrettable blind spot."[5] The commentators do not deny that Durham believed that assimilation was central, but they suggest that here, too, he had made a mistake. He was wrong, it is usually said, to propose assimilation, and doubly wrong to suppose that such measures as "responsible government" depended on it.

This is the standard opinion, the received teaching: Durham's analysis of the problems of British North America and his recommendations for reform are in general admirable, but the assimilation proposal is "regrettable," "deplorable," even infamous. In Canada this opinion has the status of a national teaching. It can be found in every textbook; it might even be said that it has become part of our political culture.

From "the perspective of our own times," argues Gerald Craig in the introduction to the most widely used edition of the Report, the assimilation proposal seems "the one great blot in an otherwise admirable and enlightened analysis."[6] Chester New, author of the standard biography of Durham, calls it "the great weakness of the Report – all the more striking because it marked Durham's only failure in the sphere of political prophecy."[7] According to R. MacGregor Dawson, in *The Government of Canada,* "Lord Durham's expectation that Quebec might come to be another weak French outpost like Louisiana ... proved in the event to be a startling miscalculation in a report conspicuous for the shrewdness and perspicacity of many of its judgements."[8] According to A.L. Burt in *The Evolution of the British Empire and Commonwealth from the American Revolution,* "the great defect of the Report is its prescription for French Canada. Durham was a false prophet and a blind reactionary when he wrote it."[9] Peter Burroughs refers to Durham's proposal for "responsible government" as "far-sighted," but argues that the assimilation proposal was the expression of "cultural chauvinism."[10] Mason Wade describes the Report as "one of the greatest studies of colonial government, and the most epoch-making state paper in Canadian history." But the principal theme of his exposition of the document is a denunciation of Durham's "racism."[11] And in "Lord Durham and the Assimilation of French Canada," William Ormsby gives his own reasons for deploring the assimilation proposal, arguing that "Durham greatly underestimated the depth and vitality of French-Canadian culture and nationalism."[12]

As I noted in the preface, it is often suggested that Durham, in the mid nineteenth century, could not have grasped the truths about nationalities and minorities obvious to us today. The implication is that he was probably no more prejudiced than others of the period. According to Burroughs, for example, "knowledge concerning cultural differences between nations was still primitive" in Durham's period.[13] Wade suggests that prejudice was "natural" to men of Durham's class.[14] And Craig argues that "Lord Durham could not know as clearly in 1839 what we know today, that it is foolhardy and naïve to speak of breaking down the customs of a well-established and organized ethnic and cultural community."[15] Even the most recent commentators maintain this approach. They are less inclined to praise the document as a whole in the extravagant terms used by the authors of twenty or thirty years ago, but they are quite as ready to condemn the assimilation proposal. In *The Durham Report and British Policy*, Ged Martin argues that because "multi-racialism" is an "important element in the modern Commonwealth," it must be said at the very least that "Durhams's attitude to the French and his proposed measures to assimilate them are at variance with the present day association." He goes on to note, in the interest of a value-free historiography, that "this is a non-historical judgement, an attempt to measure the Durham Report against twentieth century standards." But in the end he cannot refrain from indicating his disapproval any more than could his predecessors. Durham, he argues, was a "notably unfeeling example" of those Englishmen "who made no secret of their desire to hurry French Canadian separate identity into the grave."[16]

So well entrenched is this idea of the Report, so often repeated in the histories and in the classroom, that it must seem like sacrilege to call it into question. But the fact is that this view of Durham cannot be reconciled with some of the most common assumptions in modern social and political thought. When we approach the Report as a text in modern thought, focusing on the arguments and assumptions implicit in Durham's proposals, it becomes apparent that his position on assimilation is not peculiar to his century, his nation, or his class. Rather it is typical of what might be called the "mainstream" of liberal thought.[17] He will be seen, not as a chauvinist, or an English nationalist, but in characteristic liberal fashion, as a universalist. He is indeed one of those liberals who supposes that particular traditions and particular loyalties must be discarded if liberal beliefs are to be disseminated and liberal justice is to prevail. In prescribing the assimilation of the French Canadians he is not suggesting that the British should continue to dominate the French, much less that the British should have privileges denied the French. He is arguing, on the contrary, that the French Canadians must adopt the way of life prevailing on the North American continent so that they can enjoy liberal rights and freedoms on an equal footing with English-speaking Canadians.

That the advent of liberalism depends on the assimilation of disinctive ways of life is a central tenet of liberal thought. I argued in the preface that it stems ultimately from the Hobbesian and Lockean assumption of the equality of man. If all men are equal then no king can claim his throne by divine right, no religious faction claim the God-given right to govern, and no caste, clan, tribe, "race," or collectivity claim a natural right to legislate for others. Laws hiving off groups or collectivities for special treatment on the basis of religion or national origin are anathema – or so runs the classic liberal argument. It was a central idea in the nineteenth century and is still recognized in the twentieth as the heart of the liberal doctrine. In *Quebec, Social Change and Political Crisis*, Kenneth McRoberts and Dale Posgate point out, for example, that "many social scientists ... predict that the increased stress on class that comes through economic development will cause a decline of cultural and regional 'particularisms' in favour of a closer social and political integration."[18] McRoberts and Posgate themselves are uneasy with this idea; indeed their book is in large part an attempt to show the deficiencies of liberal thought in this respect. But it is because the thesis has been of signal importance in the social sciences that they have set out to question it. Among the "many social scientists" they list in connection with the idea are S.M. Lipset, Karl Deutsch, Daniel Lerner, and Lucien Pye. David Cameron is another, like McRoberts and Posgate, anxious to tackle the "mainstream" position, but again he makes no bones about its importance in twentieth-century thought: "A number of the major formal political theories which have permeated the modern world, such as liberal democracy, socialism and communism, are international and universal ... and with every major advance in one or another of these doctrines there has been an assumption that the strength of nationalist sentiment would recede."[19]

The strength of nationalist sentiment can be expected to recede, must recede, as liberalism advances: this is the heart of what I call the mainstream position. It does not suppose a dislike of particular ways of life, or hostility to minorities. Rather the proponents of the mainstream argue that without assimilation, members of nationalist minorities will be deprived of liberal benefits, and worse, will be vulnerable to political and economic exploitation of the crudest sort; they believe, in short, that assimilation is the condition for justice. As one political scientist argues: "Among most ... analysts there appears to be an agreement that a modern society is one that has a sufficient cultural homogeneity and public acceptance of common legal and social norms that rights and public policies can be made universal ... for all individuals in society without differential adjustment based on ascriptive categories or sociocultural groupings." He cites Toennies, F.X. Sutton, Talcott Parsons, Fred Riggs, David Apter, and "a host of other social scientists."[20] Without "sufficient homogeneity," without the eradication of major cleavages, liberal rights and freedoms for all cannot be established. Without "sufficient homogeneity" one group may flourish at the expense of others.

What the commentators admire in the Report, the reason for their praise for the document as a whole, is Durham's proposal for "responsible government." This is the recommendation that the colonial legislative assemblies be given the power to dismiss unresponsive ministries in the manner of the British House of Commons. It has sometimes been interpreted as a proposal for a more democratic form of government for the colonies: "By his successful recommendation of Responsible Government," argued Chester New, "Lord Durham ... created an effective Canadian democracy for all time to come."[21] And because this proposal appeared to promise the colonies a degree of independence within an enduring empire, it has also been seen as anticipating the system of relations between the home country and the senior dominions in the empire and Commonwealth of later years. "Since Lord Durham's Report," argued W.P. Morrell, "the main theme of British colonial policy has been the extension and deepening of his conception of responsible government."[22] Not all historians would describe "responsible government" in these terms, but it is fair to say that thay think of it as a liberal measure because it is a principle of self-government – in Craig's term, "the self-government of free men" – and fair to say that they praise it precisely because they see it as liberal.[23]

When they condemn the assimilation proposal, then, most commentators condemn it as illiberal. Nicholas Mansergh, for example, speaks of the "range and imaginative humanity" of Durham's political prosposals. He refers to Durham as a "radical in politics." But he insists that Durham was nonetheless "conservative and insular in respect of culture."[24] Kenneth McNaught, in *The Pelican History of Canada*, maintains that the Report's "basic constitutional liberalism ... stands in ironic relationship to its Anglo-Saxon racism."[25] W.L. Morton writes: "That Durham should have assumed so illiberal an attitude, and expressed it in the brilliant rhetoric of the Report, is not easily explained ..."[26]

But from what I have said above, it can be seen that Durham's position on French Canada is no less typically liberal than his political proposals. "Responsible government" and the assimilation proposal are expressions of the same theoretical assumptions, the same idea of political man, and the same understanding of good government. Durham rejected the idea of policies to support a distinctive French-Canadian way of life because he was convinced that such policies cannot be reconciled with liberal hopes for equality and opportunity. He believed that were the French to retain their traditional mode of life they would be exploited in a fashion no liberal could tolerate. If the French "prefer remaining stationary," he argued, "the great part of them must be labourers in the employ of English capitalists ... The evils of poverty and dependence would merely be aggravated in a ten-fold degree, by a spirit of jealous and resentful nationality, which should separate the working class of the community from the possessors of wealth and employers of labour."[27]

In fact, Durham held that the French Canadians were themselves anxious for the changes in law and policy that would enable them to compete with the English-speaking colonists in business and politics, and that in general they were eager to enjoy the rewards of life in a liberal society.[28] He did not think that the French would themselves chose to "remain stationary." He argues, as we shall see, that the conflict between the French and the English-speaking colonists had arisen in the first place because the British government had encouraged emigration from Britain and had allowed a modern commercial society to grow up beside the seigneuries, while at the same time passing laws to reinforce the old French way of life. They had followed neither of the "two modes" for dealing with a "conquered territory" consistently.[29] And as a result, he maintains, the French Canadians who tried to emulate or compete with the British had been penalized. Those who hoped to become as wealthy as the English-speaking newcomers were confined by laws inhibiting the sale of seigneurial lands, among other measures, while those who aspired to political office were denied seats in the governing councils.

Durham acknowledges at one point that the attempts of the British home-country government to follow the "first mode," that is, to "respect the rights and nationality" of the French Canadians, were meant to "conciliate" them.[30] But the result, he argues, was the rise of an English-speaking faction dedicated to "excluding" the French, and "preferring" the English.[31] In fact, he does not seem to make a clear distinction between the seemingly good-hearted attempts to "conciliate" the French by measures meant to protect their nationality, and the prejudiced practices of the English-speaking party.[32] His analysis suggests in any event that the outcome was bound to be the same. The effect of laws and policies designed to maintain the French-Canadian way of life was equally harmful whether prompted by goodwill or prejudice. The British government's periodic fits of "respect" for French-Canadian nationality had merely worked to give advantages to the English-speaking minority, advantages that group had been quick to seize.

He notes that the English-speaking settlers had few reasons to endorse laws allowing the French Canadians equal opportunity. The French might be eager to modernize, but the English, with their own interests in mind, remained adamantly opposed to their aspirations. Durham also argues that because the French party were confined to the legislative assembly – by the practices that had grown up in the years after the granting of representative institutions in 1791 – they had been virtually powerless to initiate and carry through the reforms they desired. The English, then, were striving to protect their privileged position; the French were doomed to contest in vain for equal opportunity. This, in Durham's analysis, was the source of the "fatal feud."[33] He maintained that under these conditions – it is the crux of his argument – both French and English had seen the advantages of continuing the struggle in terms of "race," that is, nationality, the English to defend their advantage and the French to challenge it. The quarrel that had begun with laws unfairly promoting the advantage of a group defined in terms of nationality had led to a contest in which both parties defined themselves by "race," and advanced their political and economic demands in the name of "race."

Other observers of French Canada at this time took what might be called the straightforwardly mainstream position that the French Canadians had abandoned all appeals to nationality as the province modernized.[34] Durham himself points out that there was much in the public posture of the French party to suggest this conclusion.[35] But it was his view that both French and English had increasingly used nationalist rhetoric, and he gives the mainstream argument the twist that will explain this fact. He does not take the French party's use of appeals to "race" to mean that the French Canadians were resisting assimilation. He suggests, on the contrary, that the increase in national feeling should be seen as an index of the very fact of assimilation. It would appear that what alarmed him most about the crisis in Lower Canada was that nationalist rhetoric had increased at the very time when both the French party leaders and the mass of the people were eager for change. The leaders of the Parti patriote spoke of "La Nation Canadienne"; they entertained "some vague expectation of absolute independence."[36] But in Durham's opinion this notion had nothing to do with a desire for a return to tradition or the maintenance of a particular way of life. These leaders were using nationalist appeals in order to secure re-election and to challenge the opposition – in themselves thoroughly modern objectives – because they were not in a position to introduce the modernizing reforms desired by the people they represented.

Durham argues, then, that assimilation was "commencing" even as the propagation of nationalist feeling escalated. In fact, his analysis suggests that the growth of national sentiment was precisely a sign that the French were assimilating. Where policies of discrimination prevail, nationalism and assimilation will increase together. And where politics is dominated by nationalist arguments, Durham suggests, the ordinary affairs of government are neglected, and confusion and even war may follow. Much of his account, as we shall see, is taken up with describing the worsening economic conditions in Lower Canada. While the French and English leaders jostled for power, the province was declining into poverty and political parties were being transformed into armies. The Rebellion of 1837 had been suppressed before Durham took office, but he knew in the summer of 1838 that hostilities were likely to break out again.

It is part of his argument, however, that these ills, for all that they ran so deep, could be remedied without difficulty. For if the problems arose from deficiencies in liberal justice – British attempts to reinforce the old French way of life; English party practices of "exclusion" – then liberal measures should heal the quarrel. The argument suggests that while it might have been necessary in the eighteenth century to render the French Canadians "entirely subordinate" to British institutions (because they were then a relatively docile people and accustomed to the autocratic rule of New France), in the nineteenth century such methods would no longer be needed because the French had shown themselves to be thoroughly familiar with British parliamentary practices, and so intolerant of measures they believed unjust that they were ready to take up arms against arbitrary authority.[37] The French were no longer a docile people, and this was perhaps the supreme mark of their assimilation.[38] In the 1830s it was not French, but English attitudes and the policies of the English-speaking party that were the problem.

If Durham's analysis is typically mainstream, so are his remedies. He proposed, in the first place, the union of the Canadas, in order to neutralise the power of the English minority in Lower Canada that had for so long tried to use the law to its own advantage. He recommended, secondly, constitutional reforms, including "responsible government," that would allow the French to aspire to government office with hope of success. His object, in short, was to place French and English on an equal footing at last.

The political constitution that he recommended with "responsible government" was described by its proponents at the time as a "balanced" or "mixed" form of government, the form established in Britain with the Glorious Revolution of 1688.[39] It was said to be the great virtue of this constitution that it prevented rule by clique and faction. It was designed to institutionalize political opposition, to ensure that there was always means to depose parties claiming supreme title to rule, even – perhaps especially – parties claiming to speak for the "nation" on the "people." For the men of 1688, the mixed constitution was the institutional remedy against rule by church hierarchy or religious faction.[40] Durham sees that it is the way to prevent an entrenched faction from ruling in perpetuity in the name of one ethnic group, the English, as English, governing the French or, indeed, the French, as French, governing the English minority. When French and English both were required to co-operate in order to obtain political advantage, parliamentary debates on economic and political issues would replace the sterile arguments about "race," and schemes for electoral victories would replace war councils.

Durham's commentators see his assimilation proposal as proof that he was prejudiced or simply ignorant of the strength of French-Canadian feeling, and thinkers like McRoberts and Posgate, and David Cameron, suggest that the rise of ethnic and nationalist demands in the world today means that liberal thought on nationalities needs revising. But Durham would say that such demands are in large part the expression of offenses against liberal principles of justice and can be remedied by liberal measures. He suggests that nationalist quarrels may characterize a modern society long after cultural differences of deep significance have disappeared. Under conditions of liberal justice, his analysis suggests, nations will grow more homogeneous in peaceful fashion. But when the "conquerors," that is, the dominant ethnic group, introduce policies to legalize cultural differences, or when they promote discriminatory appeals to "race," minority leaders in turn may find it necessary or advantageous to cloak their demands in appeals to "race," so that the rhetoric of nationality and the tendency to violence will grow even as members of the minority assimilate to the prevailing modern way of life.

In the next chapter I say more about what I have called the received opinion on the Report. I suggest that French-Canadian commentators, especially Michel Brunet, and Durham's contemporary, Etienne Parent, have perceived his intentions best. The analysis of the Report is begun in chapters three and four with a discussion of Durham's views on what we now call political culture, in order to give us a general sense of what he meant by nationalism and patriotism. I develop the argument here by means of a comparison with Alexis de Tocqueville. Although commentators have not noticed it, I am satisfied that Tocqueville was an important influence for Durham. These two European observers reached similar conclusions about the nature of politics in North America, and drew the same picture of the future of French Canada. Chapter three points out that neither Durham or Tocqueville saw any difference between the "national character" of the United States and that of the English-speaking colonies north of the border. They expected the French Canadians to assimilate to a way of life as typical of the United States and, no doubt, other modern societies, as it was of English Canada. In chapter four, I suggest why Durham would have seen the lack of religious dissension in Lower Canada as the strongest reason for supposing that the French Canadians were ready to assimilate.

Chapters five and six are devoted to Durham's thought on liberal institutions. In five, I analyse the proposal for "responsible government" as an aspect of his program for empire, and in six, as a principle of government within the colonies. It is usually said that Durham proposed a severely limited form of self-government for the colonies, and that he meant to leave the imperial parliament substantial power to legislate for the colonies. I suggest that this view stems from the same misunderstanding of liberal doctrines as the assumption that Durham was prejudiced in proposing assimilation. In fact, as a liberal, he would have been ill at ease with the idea of the home country dominating the affairs of British North America for exactly the reason that he could not accept the idea of the English in Lower Canada continuing to dominate the French. I argue that he advocated something much closer to political independence for the colonies than has usually been supposed.

Chapter six treats Durham on "responsible government" as an aspect of the mixed constitution. To show the ins and outs of his argument, I compare him to the British Radical John Arthur Roebuck, author of a lengthy proposal for the government of British North America that Durham consulted frequently. I show how Durham gave parts of Roebuck's analysis the twist that led him to conclude that nationalist appeals may escalate with assimilation. With

Durham's general position on nationality and his thought on political institutions in place, we are in a position to develop his complete argument on nationality in a liberal polity. In chapter seven, then, we have Durham's reasons for believing that attempts to support the old French way of life by law would have the effect of subjecting the French to intolerable domination, and that the best and only way to assimilate the French was to build a society of liberal rights and freedoms. Finally, chapter eight suggests ways in which Durham's conclusions might be brought into current debates about the place of French and English in Canada today. Here I address the arguments of those like McRoberts and Posgate, and David Cameron, who are dissatisfied with the position of the liberal mainstream on nationality and ethnicity.

My first object in this book is to see that Durham is recognized as a spokesman for the liberal mainstream, so that the force and coherence of his position come to light. He more often acknowledges the role of national pride and the individual's loyalty to the community than I have indicated so far. But he does not cease to argue that policies to entrench the laws and institutions of national minorities cannot be reconciled with liberal justice. To promote sharply different ways of life in a liberal society must mean denying equality and opportunity to members of the minority group in ways that they themselves will come to regard as unacceptable; it may leave them prey to ambitious leaders who will use their pride and loyalty, and their resentment at being denied equality, to exploit them in new ways. We may decide in the end that Durham and the mainstream liberals generally do not give enough place in their thought to the strength of human loyalties and the desire to be associated with a collectivity. But we cannot evaluate their argument, or our own thought on the place of national minorities in a liberal society, if we ignore their central supposition – that nationalist divisions recognized in law deny liberal rights to minorities.

CHAPTER TWO

The Report and
Its Commentators

The commentators suggest that Durham had no conception of the tenacity with which the French Canadians would cling to their way of life. "Durham, perhaps blinded by the very racism which he disowned, badly underestimated the French Canadians and their national will to life," argues Mason Wade.[1] "Lord Durham's expectation that Quebec would come to be another weak French outpost like Louisiana ... proved in the event to be startling miscalculation," writes Dawson.[2] L'Abbé Arthur Maheux suggests that Durham was misled by his reliance on the example of the assimilated minorities in the United States – the French in Louisiana and the Dutch in New York. He notes that the French Canadians "étaient plus nombreux, mieux groupés; mieux organisés grâce au système paroissial, grâce à leurs écoles." "Ils avaient pour eux la force du fait-accompli dans l'usage de leur religion, de leur langue, de leur lois civiles," he goes on; "leur forte natalité militait pour eux."[3]

For this reason, these commentators believe that Durham was surprisingly naive to suppose that such a simple measure as a bill passed by Westminster would suffice to erase the nationality of this long-established people. "The Canadian problem had long been virtually insoluble to the British," according to Ged Martin, "because the solution which they desired, that the French Canadians should cease to be disaffected, and preferably cease to be French, was beyond the reach of legislative fiat."[4] In similar fashion, G.P. de T. Glazebrook speaks of Durham's blithe conclusion that the cleavage could be legislated out of existence."[5]

Much of the discussion turns on the historians' interpretations of events in the united provinces in the 1840s and 1850s. They argue for the most part that the decisive steps to preserve French Canada were taken during these years. They suggest, as well, that what happened then was something that Durham entirely failed to foresee, and, with his prejudices and ignorance of the French-Canadian way of life, could perhaps never have foreseen.

According to William Ormsby, Durham had expected the English to club together in the united legislature, dominating the French and cowing them into submission. "Durham's whole argument", he says, "was based on the naïve assumption that the English-speaking members would act as a bloc in the united assembly. It is incredible that he could recommend responsible government and not realize that the prospect of turning out the government, on a vote of no confidence, would greatly increase the tendency towards political alignments ... In all probability, Durham ... could not conceive of any English-speaking members joining with the French."[6]

As the historians all note, the parties that formed after union were not in fact organized on ethnic or nationalist lines. Under the leadership of Robert Baldwin and Louis H. LaFontaine, the English– and French–speaking reformers joined forces to form a single party and were successful in winning office. It was this joining of forces, it is said, that enabled the French Canadians to escape English domination; it was by this means that they gained the power to protect their nationality.[7] "Canadian politicians after 1840," argues Donald Smiley, "very quickly and decisively rejected the assimilationist premises of the Durham Report."[8] As Jacques Monet puts it: "Lord Durham wanted to see the end of French Canada's nationality. But a resolute group of reformers hatched a bold scheme to frustrate his decision."[9]

Durham had proposed a legislative union, that is, a merger of the two jurisdictions, Upper and Lower Canada, under a single parliament. But the Union Act of 1840 did not follow his prescription exactly, and what actually developed in the following years was a form of association that historians sometimes refer to as "quasi-federal," or "consociational," as a way of indicating that the former provinces retained a degree of autonomy within the union. Ministerial portfolios were twinned, for example, and departments balanced so as to allow equal representation of French and English. The provincial capital rotated between the eastern and western, French and English, sectors of the province. There were attempts to establish the practice of requiring a double majority in the legislature, that is, a majority of French-speaking and a majority of English-speaking members on contentious issues.

It is Kenneth McRae's argument, based on studies of the "segmented societies" of twentieth-century Europe, that just such devices will enable a modern nation to maintain and even promote ethnic differences, while at the same time "accommodating" or reconciling differences so that national policies can be formulated in which all groups participate. Not only does he attribute the preservation of the French nationality in Canada to the emergence of "consociational" politics in the 1840s, but he also suggests that Canada was surprisingly and admirably advanced in developing such institutions.[10] Donald Smiley suggests a similar perspective when he speaks of the "very high degree of ... 'consociationalism'" attained by the reformers.[11]

No one supposes that the story ended in the 1840s. Other "bold schemes" and "resolute reformers" were needed. But few of Durham's commentators doubt the outcome. In English Canada certainly, la survivance is virtually an article of faith. To be sure, no one today is going to speak of the effects of parishes and schools, religion and birth rate in the manner of L'Abbé Arthur Maheux. It is usually suggested by contemporary authors that in some fashion Quebec has been totally transformed while remaining indubitably itself. One observer argues, for example, that the traditional nationalism of French Canada has "now almost vanished," and has been replaced by an "activist" nationalism that has developed new forms of competition with the English, challenging Ottawa in the attempt to recover powers and revenue – a nationalism, in short that "accepted the logic of social and economic modernization." [12]

In line with this view, Ormsby maintains that "French Canada evolved and it has continued to evolve." He concludes at the same time that "French Canadians are more determined than ever to preserve their separate cultural identity and to take whatever steps may be necessary to achieve that end." His own arguments in "Lord Durham and the Assimilation of French Canada" force him to admit that French Canada has adopted "social and moral values similar to those held by the Anglo-American majority in North America," and that it has become "much more materialistic in its ideals and objects." He suggests, indeed, that French Canada has "adjusted," that it has been "transformed." [13] But he makes no attempt to show how a people may retain a "separate cultural identity," while adopting "values" similar so those prevailing on the continent. In general then, although they remain vague about the present-day character of French Canada, the commentators hold that assimilation has to be ruled out. They maintain that French Canada was strong in Durham's day and is perhaps even stronger in our own. As Kenneth McRoberts and Dale Posgate put it: "The arguments as to why French Canada survived continue, but there is no denying the fact of survival." [14]

I noted in the last chapter that McRae argues for a modification or correction of liberal doctrine – a return perhaps to the "consociational politics" of the 1840s – so as to recognize in law the human desire for particularity. [15] It is sometimes suggested that membership in a collectivity virtually defines personal identity. In his essay, "Why Do Nations Have to Become States," Charles Taylor maintains that most, or all, individuals understand themselves by means of, and in terms of, their linguistic and cultural community. Their sense of their own worth depends in part on their knowledge that their community is recognized and valued by other peoples and other communities. [16] From this perspective, a doctrine that derides community and collectivity looks sinister indeed. In *Nationalism, Self-Determination and the Quebec Question,* David Cameron argues that membership in a collectivity is for many a condition of the good life: "A conception of well-being which was exhausted by the idea of material security and possession would miss much of what is most important in the life of man, and within Canada to neglect the importance of either an individual's personal autonomy or his reliance on cultural associations for the good life would be to misconstrue the animating spirit of a great many Canadians."[17]

Most historians who subscribe to the "prejudice and ignorance" view of the Report have some such understanding in mind. They assume that identification with a community defined in terms of origin, history, or tradition is a good that many or most Canadians will not relinquish, and that such collectivities – certainly the French Canadian – should be acknowledged in law. They hold that Durham was mistaken in not recognizing the stubborn vitality of ethnic groups, and mistaken, too, in not seeing that liberal societies could and should develop laws, institutions, and policies to accommodate that vitality.

In Craig's words, "Durham failed to see that Canadian development would have to be in the other direction: toward mutual respect and tolerance, towards the building of a nation based on a dual culture."[18] Wade argues that "only by the acceptance of diversity, through the understanding and reconciliation of cultural differences, can the great world problems of our time be solved."[19] Such statements suggest not only that cultural pluralism is worthwhile but that the attainment will not be difficult, that with greater "knowledge concerning cultural differences" (to use Peter Burroughs's phrase), with good will and tolerance, peoples of all backgrounds can live together, at one and the same time preserving something definitive from the different cultures, and participating in the benefits of the larger society. And from this perspective, the commentators see the proposal for assimilation as ill intentioned, perhaps even malevolent, and certainly "naïve," "ridiculous," "incredible."

The difficulties with this argument will become clearer in chapters to follow. In the first place, although the commentators suggest that he failed to understand the importance of nationality and the hold it might retain on the hearts of men in modern society, Durham himself argues in the opening pages of the document that it was in fact the peculiar merit of his analysis that he had recognized the strength of the appeal to "race" in Lower Canada. As I noted in chapter one, he argued that other observers had made the mistake of supposing that nationality no longer mattered in the province and that political measures alone would heal the quarrel. Durham portrays himself as having to convince "most minds in England" that the "peculiar and disastrous dissensions" in the colony were not simply a result of defects in the political constitution or administration, but that there existed "a far deeper and more efficient cause, – a cause which penetrated" beneath the political institutions of the colony "into its social state."[20] He had realized, and others had not, that "the contest, which had been represented as a contest of classes" was "in fact, a contest of races."[21] His analysis and prescription are valuable, he implies, exactly because he has understood that expressions of national allegiance and national hostility may continue in a modernizing society.

And because it was just this appeal to "race" that Durham deplored – the English sense that the English must club together in opposition to the French; the French sense that it was necessary to oppose the English in the name of the French nationality – it is impossible to believe, with Ormsby, that Durham hoped to see the English act as a bloc in the assembly after union. Throughout the Report he denounces English and French for clubbing together and for acting politically on the basis of nationality. In chapter seven I argue that what he meant to bring about by uniting the provinces was exactly a situation in which the English were forced to stop associating only with the English, and the French with the French. Durham desired an English majority not so that the English could dominate but so that individual figures from the former "French party" would be required to co-operate with English politicians in order to attain political office. This suggests that partnerships like that of Baldwin and LaFontaine were what he hoped to see come about. Certainly the idea of a union of the reformers of the two provinces had been in the air; Durham would have been familiar with the suggestion. He may not have foreseen the precise character of the institutions developed in the 1840s, and no doubt he would have objected to them insofar as they encouraged political organization on the basis of "race," but as we shall see, he was sure that in the end, all shared political endeavour would promote assimilation.

By way of illustrating some of the peculiarities of the English-Canadian views, we now turn to the French-speaking commentators. The picture of the Report that they give is very much at odds with that of the English Canadians. It would not be correct to suggest that the French approve of the Report or the proposal for assimilation. On the contrary, they condemn it. But they condemn it precisely because they believe it is the kind of recommendation only too likely to be effective. It is this perception, I would argue, that enables them to give a far more convincing account of Durham's position.

One of the best descriptions of what Durham was about is found in the introduction by Denis Bertrand and André Lavallée to Bertrand and Desbiens's translation of the Report:

Après avoir analysé les principaux arguments qui militent contre ou en faveur du maintien d'une collectivité canadienne-française, Durham rejette catégoriquement toute méthode de contrainte, pour appuyer une politique de lente assimilation, par la force naturelle des choses, grâce à la mise en minorité et aux autres moyens d'intégration déjà en usage en Louisiane, par le camouflage de l'égalité des droits, le mythe de l'autonomie locale, le guêpier de la législature mixte et du bilinguisme, les querelles de partis et l'émulation. L'immigration massive, la force normale d'attraction de la scène fédérale et les contraintes de l'économie auront tôt fait, ajoute-t-il, de vaincre une résistance autant désuète qu'inutile.[22]

It is tempting to argue that Bertrand and Lavallée have simply heaped at Durham's door all the forces and events in Canadian history that in their view have endangered French-Canadian nationality. But underlying their account is the perception that assimilation results from modern liberal practices and liberal justice, and in this sense their charge against Durham is faithful to his position. What prompts assimilation according to "mainstream" liberal philosophers and social scientists is exactly "la force naturelle des choses," in a system based on equality of right, with institutions promoting the co-operation of peoples of every origin and background.[23]

Durham's prescription, in the argument of Bertrand and Lavallée "laissait déjà entrevoir la Confédération et fixait, dans ses grandes lignes, la stratégie du dialogue et de la collaboration qu'allaient suivre pendant plus d'un siècle les principaux chefs du Canada anglais."[24] In similar fashion, Marcel-Pierre Hamel argues in the introduction to his 1948 translation of the Report that the centralizing trend of Canadian politics in the 1940s had come close to bringing about Durham's scheme for a legislative union of the English and French provinces, thus nearly realizing Durham's cherished project. But, he adds, "nous ne serons jamais les assimilés de la Lousisane. Demain tout recommence."[25] Like Bertrand and Lavallée, Hamel is hostile but far from seeing Durham's proposals as "foolhardy" or ridiculous.

The most crucial commentator from our point of view was Durham's contemporary, Etienne Parent, editor of *Le Canadien*, who published a series of articles on the Report immediately after it appeared. What was most striking about Parent's reaction was that in response to the argument he found in the Report, he at first endorsed the idea of assimilation. He had always been an ardent supporter of liberal principles of government, and he accepted outright the idea that to adopt liberal principles would mean abandoning nationality.[26] In October 1839, he wrote: "Les Canadiens Français n'ont plus rien à attendre...pour leur nationalité. Que leur reste-t-il donc à faire dans leur propre intérêt et dans celui de leurs enfants, si ce n'est de travailler eux-mêmes de toutes leurs forces à amener une assimilation qui brise a barrière qui les sépare des populations que les environnent de toutes parts." The article opens with a plea for "responsible government" as expounded by Lord Durham and Joseph Howe, and ends with a picture of the great and powerful liberal nation that will arise on the banks of the St Lawrence after the French have made the necessary sacrifice.[27] (Hamel complained, "Etienne Parent lui aussi eut un terrible moment de faiblesse."[28])

Almost immediately, however, Parent set out to try to reconcile the insight he had taken from the Report with his own hopes for the survival of the French-Canadian nationality, and the great interest of his work lies in this endeavour. But we cannot suppose that his acceptance of assimilation was simply a result of a failure of will or intelligence. That would make nonsense of everything he wrote on the subject of nationality, for he himself claimed that his initial acceptance of the proposal was based on his previous understanding of the nature of liberal political institutions, while his later articles must be seen as attempts to resolve this understanding with his desire to see pride in nationality remain for the French Canadians. He argued, in the end, that French nationality might be preserved in a federal union of all the British North American colonies, but the character of his debate with himself on this subject shows that he never turned his back on the fundamental idea he had derived from the Report or found confirmed there: that there is something problematic about the supposition that nationalism and liberalism may be easily reconciled.

The best known of Durham's French-speaking commentators today is Michel Brunet. Ramsay Cook notes that

Durham's views, which infuriate most French Canadians, exercise a peculiar magnetism on Brunet, who once called the English lord "the best historian of Canada." Brunet seems torn between two alternatives: on the one hand is the suspicion that Durham was accurate in his analysis of the causes of the 1837 affair and therefore right in his prescription of assimilation; on the other is his nationalist commitment to *la survivance*. Brunet the social scientist attempts to use Durham's analysis without reaching the conclusions that are repugnant to Brunet the nationalist.[29]

Cook's own writings do not follow the received tradition in the matter of the Durham Report; while Brunet's treatment of the proposal for assimilation on the level of theory, that is, as a problem or challenge rather than a "deplorable error" or "startling miscalculation," is far indeed from the usual textbook picture.

Behind the arguments of Parent, who settles for federalism, and Brunet, who hopes for independence, lies the same insight, I believe. Both know there is much to be valued in the liberal regime – above all, the famous liberal guarantees of equality, rights, and freedoms. But both know as well that it is exercise of these principles that wears away particular national loyalties. It is just this understanding that enables them to interpret Durham so well. They have recognized the liberal character and the weight of his position on nationality as English-speaking commentators have not.

English-Canadian commentators may believe that only ignorance and prejudice stands in the way of a thorough-going dualism or multiculturalism – that goodwill and "knowledge concerning cultural differences" will win the day. But the French are far more sceptical. From their more philosophical position, the problem looks less tractable. And as for goodwill, tolerance, and the mutual participation of French and English together in the affairs of the nation – these are, they suggest, Durham's very remedies.

It is surprising that the English-speaking historians have so misread the Report. Their mistake, as I have suggested, results largely from not putting Durham in the context of British political philosophy and modern social science. But it has been easier for them to pronounce judgment, I believe, because they have seen themselves as modelling their views on those of respected Englishmen of the turn of the century.

After the 1840s, until the turn of the century, the Report was seldom studied closely. As Ged Martin notes, Durham was often cited in public debates, but the references are best described as "decorative or honorific."[30] In the decade after 1900 – the years of the South African crisis – attention focused sharply on him again.[31] Many observers wondered if his famous proposal for assimilation would prove appropriate tor the new Dutch subjects. However, prominent historians of the time believed that plans to assimilate the Dutch were ill founded. And they were quite as ready to argue that Durham had erred in proposing assimilation for the French.

These Edwardian views at first sight resemble those of later writers. Indeed, as I have suggested, we can trace the clichés about Durham to this point. H.E. Egerton's observation, from the introduction to *Canadian Constitutional Documents*, is typical: "The time-spirit has dealt summarily with one of the main tenets of Durham's political belief – the view that it was necessary to absorb the French national character in a dominant Anglo-Saxon type."[32] C.P. Lucas, whose discussion of the Report in the introductory volume of his 1912 edition is the most comprehensive of the time, writes: "Whether in Canada, or in South Africa, the only policy which is ... consistent with British traditions and instincts, is to let the different languages run their course side by side.[33] A closer examination, however, reveals fundamental differences.

The Canadian and English historians of a later generation oppose the idea of assimilation because they wish to see the French in Canada remain French. The Edwardians, in contrast, writing at the height of the empire, were chiefly concerned to see that the British remained purely British. Lucas notes, for example, that Durham "advocated change of language in order to raise a particular dependency from the status of dependence to that of self-government."[34] But his own suggestion, that it is better "to let the languages run side by side," points to the idea that it might be preferable to let the French Canadians remain dependent. In this vein he argues that Durham's recommendation ran counter to the "British instinct of fair play and generosity to the conquered, which after all is nearly the most valuable asset that a ruling race can possess."[35]

Egerton is more explicit. He believed that the British had a "nationhood," that is, an imperial mission that set them apart.[36] His vision of empire has a multicultural dimension, it is true. He pictures the British Empire as a mosaic, for example, and no more than later Canadians who use the same image does he wish to see the various components lose their distinctive characteristics. But he develops the metaphor as no later writer would. The empire, he suggests, is "an elaborate mosaic, wherein, side by side with the Empire of India, Dominion, Commonwealth, self-governing colony, Crown colony, chartered company, Protectorate, sphere of influence, adds each its lustre to the pavement which is ever being trod by fresh generations of our race as they pass to and fro."[37] It is for the British, then, to rule. This is their "nationhood," one in which the subordinate peoples of the empire are not to participate. The French in this analysis, would remain distinctively French only so long as they refrained from participating with the British in the great affairs proper to the British "race."

The Edwardian argument, it must be noted, turns on the same observation as Durham's: participation assimilates. Durham believed that in a society offering equal opportunity for all, assimilation was inevitable. But Lucas and Egerton, unhampered by the doctrine of equal opportunity, were able to argue that some tasks of government and empire were simply inappropriate for the French Canadians, and it was on this basis that they rejected assimilation.

Brunet and Parent, too, are cognizant of the supposition that with "responsible government," with equal opportunity, the corrosive forces of assimilation are let loose. It is only the English Canadians who are all at sea. They have taken the idea of cultural pluralism from their Edwardian mentors, but married it to the liberal view of participation and equality. They wish to see the French-Canadian nationality retain its lustre while at the same time ensuring French Canadians perfect political equality. The idea is sympathetic, but from the perspective of the liberal mainstream, simplistic.

CHAPTER THREE

Durham and Tocqueville on Society

"On ne peut se dissimuler que la race anglaise n'ait acquis une immense prépondérance sur toutes les autres races européennes du nouveau monde," wrote Tocqueville. "Elle leur est très supérieure en civilisation, en industrie et en puissance."[1] He speaks of the English as superior in "civilisation," industry, and power. Durham argues that "the French are not so civilized, so energetic, or so money-making a race as that by which they are surrounded."[2] In all likelihood Durham had the first volume of Tocqueville's *De la Démocratie en Amérique* open before him as he wrote in the winter of 1838–9. He borrowed Tocqueville's ideas and tone and even copied phrases. Tocqueville was well known in England and the first volume of *De la Démocratie* was widely read when it came out in 1835. Any number of Durham's acquaintances, whig or Radical, could have directed his attention to Tocqueville's remarks on Canada.[3]

Like Durham, Tocqueville maintains that the assimilation of the French in Canada is both inevitable and good: "À une époque que nous pouvons dire prochaine, puisqu'il s'agit ici de la vie des peuples, les Anglo-Américains couvriront seuls tout l'immense espace compris entre les glaces polaires et les tropiques; ils se répandront des grèves de l'océan Atlantique jusqu'aux rivages de la mer du Sud".[4] But it is impossible in Tocqueville's case to suppose that he accepts the idea of assimilation out of anti-Gallic prejudices – "racial and imperialist biases" – a preference for England and the English. When his position is amplified, it will be seen that insofar as he endorses the liberal institutions he found in the United States, he, too, is a spokesman for the liberal mainstream on nationality.

In Tocqueville's work Durham found, I suggest, a view of life in North America and conclusions about the future of the French that fitted with and extended his own perspective. Tocqueville might be seen as more philosophical: although he begins, like Durham, with the discussion of concrete problems, he more often draws out the universal precepts suggested by the analysis.

He sees farther into the future and is more cognizant of the value of past institutions. Durham, in comparison, appears more optimistic, even complacent about the rewards of liberal society. On the whole, however, their views are remarkably similar. The comparison will help to point to the larger teaching behind Durham's proposals for British North America.

Tocqueville's conclusions about French Canada are the more striking because they were the product of a radical change of mind. His surprise and delight on first encountering the French in North America are recorded in his journal. He and his travelling companion Beaumont visited Lower Canada in the fall of 1832, and for a time they seem to have looked forward to the re-establishment of the French nation in the New World. It seemed to Tocqueville at this point, moreover, that the persistence of the French way of life under British rule called in question the idea that mankind was advancing toward unity and the world becoming more homogeneous.[5] In one entry in his travel journal, for example, we see him entertaining the idea that nature had given each people an indelible national character.[6]

But at some point between 1832 and 1835, he changed his mind. He argued that the assimilation of the French in Canada had been delayed, but was nevertheless certain:

Il arrivera donc un temps où l'on pourra voir dans l'Amérique du Nord cent cinquante millions d'hommes égaux entre eux, qui tous appartiendront à la même famille, qui auront le même point de départ, la même civilisation, la même langue, la même religion, les mêmes habitudes, les mêmes mœurs, et à travers lesquels la pensée circulera sous la même forme et se peindra des mêmes couleurs. Tout le reste est douteux, mais ceci est certain. Or, voici un fait entièrement nouveau dans le monde.[7]

The conclusion surely gains force from the fact of his earlier speculations. When his English translator, Henry Reeve, wrote just after the outbreak of the 1837 rebellions to ask for Tocqueville's views on this new development – hoping perhaps that he would announce his approval of the British Radical party's support for the patriote cause – he replied that he could only advise the French to throw in their lot with the English.[8]

In the near future, Tocqueville argues, "les Anglo-Américains se répandront des grèves de l'océan Atlantique jusqu'aux rivages de la mer du Sud." Durham writes: "I entertain no doubts as to the national character which must be given to Lower Canada; it must be that of ... the majority of the population of British America; that of the great race which must, in the lapse of no long period of time, be predominant over the whole North American Continent."[9] He has changed the mood from prediction to prescription, but retained Tocqueville's suggestion that the process of assimilation is already under way and is inevitable.

The following passages lead to the core of Durham's position: that the

French are not so "civilized, so energetic or so money-making a race"; and that the English will be predominant over the whole of the North American continent. He writes as if anticipating the objections of later commentators:

It may be said that this is a hard measure to a conquered people; that the French were originally the whole, and still are the bulk of the population of Lower Canada; that the English are new comers, who have no right to demand the extinction of the nationality of a people, among whom commercial enterprize has drawn them. It may be said, that, if the French are not so civilized, so energetic, or so money-making a race as that by which they are surrounded, they are an amiable, a virtuous, and a contented people, possessing all the essentials of material comfort, and not to be despised or ill-used, because they seek to enjoy what they have, without emulating the spirit of accumulation, which influences their neighbours. Their nationality is, after all, an inheritance; and they must be not too severely punished, because they have dreamed of maintaining on the distant banks of the St. Lawrence, and transmitting to their posterity, the language, the manners, and the institutions of that great nation, that for two centuries gave the tone of thought to the European Continent. [10]

For the most part Durham and Tocqueville use "civilization" to refer only to modern commercial societies. In the introduction to volume one, for example, Tocqueville speaks of the Europeans who opposed liberal democracy in his day as the adversaries of "civilisation." [11] In another instance he refers to the Italians, Spaniards, and Portuguese of this period as less "civilized" than the English because they have not been as forward in producing articles of consumption. [12] Throughout the two volumes of *De la Démocratie* he is concerned to show the commercial character of life in the United States. "L'homme du peuple, aux États-Unis," he argues in one passage, "a compris l'influence qu'exerce la prospérité générale sur son bonheur ... il travaille au bien de l'État ... par cupidité." [13] It is this society of the greedy that he calls "civilized." Similarly Durham in a typical passage, refers to the United States as characterized by "productive industry, increasing wealth, and progressive civilization." In another he links "industrial progress" and "civilization." [14] He describes the English as "civilized" in short because – to use the phrase from the passage above – they are the "money-makers."

In Durham's depiction, then, the English are "civilized," but not "virtuous," or "contented" like the French. Democratic man, argues Tocqueville, "n'est ni plus vertueux ni plus heureux peut-être, mais plus éclairé et plus actif que ses devanciers." [15] Durham describes the English labourers of Lower Canada as "demoralized," in constrast to the French of the same social rank who are said to be "well-ordered" – meaning, as the context indicates, morally ordered. [16] The French, if not "civilized," are "virtuous." He notes that under British rule – and to the shame of the British – the French had been deprived of the institutions that would have elevated them to "freedom and civilization."[17] But he describes them as "kindly, frugal, industrious and honest."[18]

The old French regime he depicts as a society that directed men to virtue, a society in which men were held accountable to standards of conduct ascribed ultimately to God. In such a society, public order will result from habitual obedience to rulers and deity. So Durham describes the French Canadians of former days as "mild" and "inactive."[19] It was true, as all could see in the 1830s, that the character of life in the province had begun to change. The French Canadians in arms against the British were no longer the docile folk of 1760. And in Durham's view this was evidence of their assimilation.[20] Yet he would seem to have believed that something still remained of the old French "manners," and that the French still possessed a sense of virtue that went beyond mere prudent self-interest.[21]

Democratic man is more "active," says Tocqueville. Durham speaks of the English settlers in British North America as "turbulent," "intelligent," "energetic."[22] He often speaks of the "independence" of the citizen as a crucial factor in modern society, referring to it at times as a condition for liberal government, and at times as one of the benefits. On the campaign trail in Britain, for example, he commended one Scottish borough for exercising its new franchise with "independence and public advantage" – suggesting that it is the individual voter's independent establishment of his own objects that yields public advantage.[23] In another instance he characterized the movement for parliamentary reform in Britain as "the struggle of independence against power."[24] In the society of "freedom and civilization," political obligation, at best, will be based on each man's prudent understanding that his own interests are more likely to be gratified by "large" programs than by "narrow" ones, that is by programs tending to include the interests of many or all in society.[25] It may be noted that Tocqueville, like Durham, speaks of the Anglo-Americans as more "intelligent." But neither believes "intelligence," "energy," or "enlightenment" to be native characteristics. By "intelligence," for example, they always mean the kind of political shrewdness that results from participating in elections or policy making.[26] The French will quickly become as "intelligent" in this sense as the English.

Both writers, then, view "civilization" as the way of life soon to be dominant everywhere on the continent, a society in which political institutions are firmly based on the individual's self-seeking desires. The English, in their description, could be said to represent "modernity," and the French, or rather the French as they had been, "tradition." Neither uses these terms in exactly the sense suggested here; nevertheless, as I noted in chapter one, we may say that Durham's thought, and Tocqueville's, is in line with that school of politics that thinks in terms of "traditional" and "modern." Durham refers to the French Canadiens as they were in the years after the conquest, as constrained by "ancient prejudices, ancient customs and ancient laws." He speaks of French Canada as an "old and stationary society in a new and progressive world."[27] In this vein, too, he refers to the institutions of the French before 1760 as a "repressive despotism."[28] Tocqueville writes: "Les Français du Canada ... ont fidèlement conservé les traditions des anciennes mœurs."[29]

Undoubtedly, in true liberal style, Durham preferred the modern to the traditional, the regime of freedom to the regime of "virtue." He valued the modern because he valued freedom, and because he believed that free institutions would result in prosperity. Indeed, in the case of French Canada he argues that the introduction of a modern, reformed constitution is the only way to avoid mass poverty. That he regarded the modern way as more dignified is suggested by his use of the word "elevated" in a passage we have already noted: "The continued negligence of the British government left the mass of the people without any of the institutions which would have elevated them in freedom and civilization."[30] Freedom, "independence," and prosperity are the promises of the modern way of life. As the owner of Lambton Collieries, one of England's largest coal-mining enterprises, he knew the poverty, misery, and vice – the demoralization – that characterized the lives of many people under England's free institutions.[31] The habitants of Quebec were far more prosperous than Durham's own tenants and employees. Nevertheless, he is convinced that the habitant's future holds increasing poverty, and the English citizen's, increasing wealth.[32]

We cannot conclude that Durham saw nothing worthwhile in the old French-Canadian way of life. Only those who feel contempt themselves for the "old and stationary," and the "ancient," will suppose that he used these terms pejoratively. According to Peter Burroughs, Englishmen of Durham's time were "convinced of the inherent superiority of British institutions and traditions."[33] But Durham did not suppose that the English way of life was superior in producing virtue or happiness, and he knew very well that it was the "ancient laws and prejudices" of the French Canadians that gave the labourers their "well-ordered" character and the society in general its contentment.

There is undoubtedly a note of nostalgia in the long passage cited above, and this surely derives from Tocqueville, who was in all ways less sanguine about liberal democracy and more alert to the value of aspects of tradition. But I suggest that Durham could see something of the truth behind Tocqueville's respect for the old ways of life: he would not have been the only governor of French Canada to wonder, if only briefly, whether institutions promoting virtue and happiness might not be preferable to institutions grounded on the "money-making" motive and the "spirit of accumulation."[34]

Neither writer, then, thought of the English "race" as representing a particularity; neither was proposing that the French Canadians renounce the habits, "manners," and "mode of life" of one particularity in order to adopt the mode of life of another. Rather they depict the English "race" as standing for modernity, the "universal and homogeneous" society of the future.[35] Both were struck, for example, by the similarities between the societies north and south of the Canadian border. The English population of the Canadas, and the inhabitants of the northern states of the Union, Durham argues, "speak the same language, live under laws having the same origin, and preserve the same customs and habits." These are, he says, two divisions of an "identical population."[36] Tocqueville, using the terms that, as it appears, Durham borrowed, describes the English "population" of the British colonies as "identique à celle des États-Unis."[37] By speaking of the assimilation of the French to the British way of life, Durham and Tocqueville mean to indicate that the French must move from a particular to the universal society.

To see Durham's thought on that future way of life – the society of "freedom and civilization" – we must turn to three extended arguments in the Report where he suggests the rewards the colonists can look forward to, once his reforms have been adopted. If the French are to give up their nationality, their dream of "maintaining on the distant banks of the St. Lawrence ... the language, the manners and the institutions" of old France, what can they expect in return? The first argument is found in the passages dealing with what he calls the "mortifying contrast" between the northeastern United States, and the British colonies on the other side of the border. Durham suggests that although the British North Americans were presently suffering from a severe economic depression, they could yet hope to enjoy a prosperity comparable to the American if his advice were followed. The second argument can be seen in his discussion of the process of assimilation in Louisiana; he suggests that assimilation was the choice of the French populace of the American state and brought with it substantial benefits. And the third is found in his musings about the possibility of the several colonies of British North America joining together to form one union in a "counterbalance" to the United States.

Durham returns again and again to a picture of the blooming prosperity of the New England states, always contrasting it with the depressed conditions prevailing to the north. In one passage he speaks of the "spirit of American progress" as something that the British colonists should emulate; in another he refers to the "rapid progress of the [American] people in material comfort and social improvement."[38] On the American side of the border, he argues, "all is activity and bustle." Every year, "numerous settlements are formed, and thousands of farms are created out of the waste." "Good houses, warehouses, mills, inns, villages, towns and even great cities, are almost seen to spring up out of the desert."[39] The "rapid progress" of the American communities in this depiction appears to depend above all on the "ways of communication and transport," the systems of canals, roads, railways, harbours, bridges, and wharves – in short, access to markets. What he sees in the northern United States, in other words, is a flourishing commercial society, the way of life that the "money-making race" would choose. But we might note that along with the "ways of communication," the banks and warehouses, there were schools, township buildings, bookstores, court-houses – and fine churches.[40]

North of the border, in contrast, the populace is "widely scattered" in the forest, "without towns and markets, almost without roads," living in mean houses and drawing little more than a rude subsistence from ill-cultivated land.[41] "There is but one railroad in all British America," he notes, and "that ... is only 15 miles long." He points out that land values were falling in the British provinces: "On this side the line a very large extent of land is wholly unsaleable while on the other side property is continually changing hands." But perhaps the most striking index of poor conditions in British North America in his view was the high "re-emigration" rate.[42] Men long settled in the provinces, or, perhaps even more telling, recent immigrants from Britain, were leaving for the United States in large numbers. Able and energetic men were choosing to live under a different administration.

The "mortifying contrast" is a reproach levelled at the imperial government. Durham assumes that material prosperity is the consequence of good political institutions. Commerce will flourish only under good laws, perhaps only under conditions of self-government. The British colonists were poor not because they were inadequate farmers, or because the soil was inferior, but because they lived under deficient institutions.[43] In one passage he uses the "mortifying contrast" to point out the folly of failing to provide adequate schools; in another, the problems attendant on the refusal to provide municipal institutions.[44] Without schools and without political experience at the local level, "intelligence" and "industry" will flag. But the principal cause of the contrast, he argues, was to be found in the British system of disposing of wild lands. The practices followed in British North America, in his view, were in all ways inferior to the American. The imperial government typically granted tracts of frontier land in what he describes as a highly arbitrary fashion. Many of the new landholders refused to live on the land, or were in no position to take up residence, with the result that cultivated areas might be separated by miles of wilderness. "Deserts are thus interposed between the industrious settlers; the natural difficulties of communication are greatly enhanced ... the cultivator is cut off or far removed from a market."[45]

But if Durham levels a reproach at the British administration in these passages, he means at the same time to hold out a promise to the colonists. His praise of American conditions is by no means intended to suggest that American political institutions are absolutely superior. It is true that in one passage he refers to the American form of government as "eminently responsible."[46] It was, no doubt, a form of government under which a liberal man might choose to live. But it is his purpose in the passages describing the "mortifying contrast" to persuade the colonists of British North America that under a reformed British constitution, prosperity to equal or exceed the American could yet be theirs.

In this connection he puts forward what was seen by many Englishmen at the time, among them Durham's associates on the Canada mission, as a British scheme – that is, a scheme compatible with parliamentary institutions and imperial connection – that had all the advantages of the American frontier regulations.[47] The scheme had originated with Edward Gibbon Wakefield, and had been promulgated by colonial reform groups with which Durham had been associated before he turned to Canadian affairs.[48] It forms an integral part of Durham's argument, although it is not always treated as such by his commentators. The Wakefield plan called for the controlled sale of new lands – as opposed to outright grants – and the emigration of entire communities from the home country. It was intended to prevent absentee landlordism and to concentrate the population so as to prevent or correct just such a checkered pattern of land use as had developed in Upper Canada and the Maritime provinces. There was to be a slow and orderly expansion of the frontier, leaving no settlement or community cut off from the commercial centre.

As I argue in chapter five, Durham assumes that the colonists on the advent of self-government will see it as advantageous to promote co-operation with the home country in a scheme of orderly land use and immigration. It was vital, in his opinion, that the British government refrain from using grants of land in the colonies to reward political favourites. It was just as important that the colonies and home country co-operate in the settlement of the vast new territories of North America, and this he fully expected after "responsible government." Durham's proposals would mean, then, that north of the border, as in the south, new villages, towns, and great cities would spring up out of the desert, and that British North America would at last begin to develop the markets, experience, and the progress typical of its neighbour.

The message is directed to the French as well as the English: although most of the passages cited above form part of his discussion of the failure of land-administration policies in the colonies, Durham repeats the argument, in much the same form, as a preface to the whole of the concluding section of the Report; in this position it precedes his most comprehensive statement of the argument for assimilation.[49] I noted in the last chapter that some of Durham's commentators have expressed surprise that he could expect by a simple political measure such as the union of the Canadas – "legislative fiat" – to change the national character of a people.[50] But if we consider the assimilation proposal in conjunction with his picture of American progress, we must suppose that Durham expects his proposal to be acceptable exactly because he can argue that liberal society offers such rewards.

It is this idea that lies behind the conviction of both Durham and Tocqueville that the dominance of modern liberalism was inevitable in North America. Given the opportunity, they suggest, all men, whatever their origins, will put their desire for prosperity before traditional loyalties. It is easier, it is more "natural," that is, more in accord with man's fundamental inclinations, to strive for wealth than to accept the discipline of institutions that promote virtue, even contentment, but reward with poverty. So Durham speaks of the "natural and necessary termination" of the quarrel between French and English, and argues that the French "when once placed, by the legitimate course of events and the working of natural causes, in a minority, would abandon their vain hope of nationality."[51] His simple measure would suffice because it depended on the commonest of human desires. In the long run, dreams of nationality must fail; the French will not maintain the old way of life, nor can the English long respect French hopes. The "money-making race" will dominate because all will become money-makers. The French, too, will be money-makers, liberal, "English."

Louisiana afforded Durham a complete description of the process. He notes that many Englishmen in Lower Canada had believed that the federal govern-ment in the United States had used harsh and even violent means to sweep away the French laws and language in the state.[52] His summary of affairs in Louisiana is meant to demonstrate the falsity of that picture. Assimilation in the United States, he argues, was not accomplished by force and not brought about directly by the English-speaking majority. Rather it was the result of a multitude of decisions in the French community. The change of law, he argues, "effected in the manner most consonant to the largest views of legis-lation, was not forced on the legislature and the people of the State by an external authority, but was the suggestion of their own political wisdom."[53]

He suggests that jealousy, understandably enough, was the first response of the French to the influx of the English into the area, and to the initially greater success of the English in their business undertakings. But he main-tains that under conditions of perfectly free competition, the French were moved by their jealousy to adopt the way of life that would secure them the same economic advantages.

The educated and ambitious among the French were offered the highest prize of liberal society, that is, power and position in the government of a large and important nation.

The eye of every ambitious man turned naturally to the great centre of federal affairs, and the high prizes of federal ambition ... The legislation and government of Loui-siana were from the first insignificant, compared with the interests involved in the discussions at Washington. It became the object of every aspiring man to merge his French, and adopt completely an American nationality.[54]

In this way the competitive but peaceful process of assimilation began.

The two languages remained in use in the state legislature, he notes. Newspapers were printed in both languages. The two systems of law were digested into a common code.[55] He speaks of the "amalgamation" of the laws – a term Tocqueville also uses in describing Louisiana.[56] But evidently no French laws were to remain that would impede commercial progress.

In a sense, the French of Louisiana were "English" as soon as they entered competition; they joined the money-makers with the first promptings of jealousy. And the necessary consequence, Durham argues, was that the "French language and manners bid fair, in no long time, to follow their laws, and pass away like the Dutch peculiarities of New York."[57] Under these easy and "natural" conditions, the French of Louisiana adopted the way of life, language, and "manners" prevailing on the continent.

Not force then, but liberal justice, that is, equal opportunity for all in public and in commercial activities, is the means to this end. Louisiana, in Durhams's opinion, exemplified the "influence of perfectly equal and popular institutions in effacing distinctions of race without disorder or oppression."[58] As Bertrand and Lavallée suggest, "le camoflage de l'égalité des droits ..., le guêpier du bilinguisme" are the effective means – the liberal means – to a liberal end.[59]

That there were other ways by which rulers might try to assimilate minorities, Durham knew very well. In 1832 he was appointed ambassador to Russia. His general instructions from Palmerston included, among other matters, a review of the Polish question.[60] It was understood that he could do no more than remonstrate mildly with the Russians over the abrogation of the Polish constitution, but so that he might be informed as to the extent of the Russian incursion, Palmerston noted that "statements have reached this government which if true, tend to show a deliberate intention on the part of the Russian government, to break down the nationality of Poland, and deprive it of everything which either in outward form or general substance gives to its people the character of a separate nation." He goes on to list specific measures:

The abolition of Polish Colours; the introduction of the Russian language into publick acts, the removal to Russia of the national library, and publick collections ... the suppression of schools and other establishments for publick instruction; the removal of a great number of children to Russia on the pretense of educating them at the publick expense; the transportation of whole families to the interior of Russia; the extent and severity of the military conscription, the large introduction of Russians into the public employments in Poland, the interference with the National Church ...[61]

Gerald Craig considers Durham's assimilation proposal a wish to "break down" the French-Canadian nationality. Peter Burroughs says Englishmen attempted to "destroy" French Canada.[62] Such language would be appropriate for the czar's attempt to crush the Poles. But to use it of Durham's program obscures the gentle and attractive character of the liberal way to assimilation – and its far more potent threat.

Nevertheless, we may ask if Durham said nothing of what we usually regard as common human feelings – love of homeland, attachment to traditions, patriotism. We see his thought on these matters most clearly in his picture of the future union of the British North American colonies. A glance through the Report, in fact, shows terms like "patriotism" "pride," and "attachment" adorning many pages.

Although Durham rejected the idea of a union of all the colonies for the immediate future, and believed that it was of the greatest importance to unite the two Canadian provinces as soon as possible, he did not entirely abandon the idea of a united British North America. He hoped that in time the union of the Canadas would expand into a legislative union – not a federation – of the several colonies, to form, as he said, "something like a national existence," a "counterbalance" on the continent to the presence of the United States.[63]

The new national existence would be British in name and have parliamentary institutions. Durham speaks of the "feelings," "sentiments," and "attachment" of the British subjects of North America for these institutions. This attachment, he suggests, already existed and could be used to assist in building the future North American nation. He argues that the colonists in that new nation would feel "affection for the mother country," and pride in the glories of the British empire and in the signs of Britain's power.[64]

All this sounds at first as if he were granting to the English-speaking colonists what he denied to the French – the capacity to maintain loyalty and attachment as enduring sentiments. He appears to be promoting English patriotism and disallowing French. But the larger context shows that his teaching here is consistent with his discussion of the motives that would lead the French to relinquish their nationality. For the hypothetical picture of the future loyalty of the British North Americans is given as part of his discussion of the very real disloyalty of many of the colonists at the very time he was writing. In his view sentiment, loyalty, attachment, had not in fact proved of great importance for the English in the colonies. On the contrary, as he noted, many had immigrated to the United States and others had thrown over patriotic feelings altogether and were proposing to join the colonies to the American union.[65] They had exhibited little loyalty to their British North American governments and less to Britain.

It is worth noting that Durham dwells at length on the evidence of colonial disloyalty. To be sure, the rebellions of 1837 had been of some importance; it is hardly surprising that he returns often to this subject. But the fact is that Durham uses the discussion of disloyalty in part for effect, as he did the picture of American prosperity. The latter held out the promise of rewards for the colonists if they chose British institutions. The discussion of disloyalty, in contrast, has the character of a threat and is surely addressed to the British government. If his reforms are not passed, he implies, colonial revolution and abrupt independence will ensue. At the same time, he provides a vision of a future pacific "national existence," loyal to the mother country, to assure the home government that the colonists are capable of patriotism under the right conditions.

The device he uses in these passages is one he employed with effect in the debates in the British Parliament at the time of the Great Reform Bill. Speaking of the riots and protests that marked that period, he would describe in glowing terms the general loyalty of the English populace, while at the same time warning the tories of more riots to come if the reform measure was not passed.[66] The device gains from its seeming contradiction, but owes its real punch to the fact that from the liberal perspective, simple truth lies behind it. Attachment and loyalty, according to Durham, are always grounded in the gratification of personal and economic interests. A "general sense of obligation to the Government," results when legislation favours "the most rapid progress of the people in material comfort and social improvement."[67] The English rioters would become informed and loyal electors when they were allowed to vote. The colonists' loyalty to the British North America of the future, and their allegiance to the home country, would be the stronger because they had the kind of lively perception of their own interests that in 1837 had prompted disloyalty.

Only if reforms to promote self-government and economic progress were forthcoming, then, would the colonists continue to call themselves British. Only if the colonies were granted something close to political independence would the imperial connection retain force. Discontent and irritation will always weaken "affection," he argued.[68] Pride in the glories of British power will never be enough for the ambitious colonist who has been deprived of a place in the governing councils of his own land.[69]

As for the British North American union of the future, it would be in his words a "united and homogeneous" society.[70] But it would not be, at bottom, sentiment, patriotism, or pride in history that would unify and support the new nation, nor language, customs, and "manners." Doubtless all the inhabitants of the new British North America would speak of, and feel, national loyalty and pride. They would assuredly know one "mode of life" and perhaps speak one language. But their national pride would reflect chiefly their satisfaction with a state that promoted the general good by means of institutions furthering individual comforts and careers. In short, he gives exactly the same exposition of the springs of political action and loyalty in his description of the future colonial union, as he did in his analysis of the assimilation of the French in Louisiana.

The kind of loyalty that Durham attributes to the citizens of the future union,

Tocqueville would call rational, well considered. Tocqueville describes two kinds of patriotism. One is disinterested and instinctive. "Cet amour instinctif se confond avec le goût des coutumes anciennes, avec le respect des aïeux et la mémoire du passé." The other is "plus rationnel que celui-là; moins généreux, moins ardent peut-être, mais plus fécond et plus durable."[71] It is grounded on personal interest: "Un homme … sait que la loi lui permet de contribuer à produire ce bien-être, et il s'intéresse à la prospérité de son pays, d'abord comme à une chose qui lui est utile, et ensuite comme à son ouvrage."[72] He maintains that the day for the first kind of patriotism is past. If it was a grander, more brilliant sentiment, it cannot be achieved – or, it may be, cannot be allowed – in modern society.

Tocqueville argues that it would be wrong to mistake our modern well-considered patriotism for the feeling men knew in former days, but he suggests that it would also be wrong to suppose that our own milder sentiments are without value.

Durham, as well, does not altogether deny the existence of patriotic feelings in the society of "freedom and civilization." The pride that New Englanders felt in their banks, courthouses, township buildings and churches, and that the British North Americans will feel in the institutions of that new "national existence" north of the border is not supported by a distinctive way of life, but it is pride of a kind. Unlike Tocqueville, he does not argue that this pride is durable. He has reason to stress the fact that it blooms only with prosperity and fades with adversity.

In some passages, moreover, he suggests that for a few men patriotic feelings may indeed override personal interest. He argues in one instance that "patriotism" may deter "calm" men from acting with a party in opposition to national objects, where only "prudence," that is, enlightened self-interest, restrains the "timid."[73] Some men may cherish strong feelings of community and homeland. The loss of nationality that he predicted for the French was a real loss for some. If it was, as he believed, inevitable, it might nevertheless be regretted.

Liberalism may indeed underestimate the strength of real patriotism and nationalist feeling. But it does not argue that there are no such sentiments. Tocqueville tells us why we must chose and defend modern liberal institutions. Nevertheless, his description of the loyalty and patriotism of past societies is an antidote to undue satisfaction with liberalism. Durham tells us why the French had to chose the continental way of life. But he reminds us briefly of the merits of the regime of virtue. The promotion of distinctive minority ways of life within the larger nation was rejected by mainstream thinkers, not because they were ignorant of these feelings, but because they believed that political recognition of nationalities within the liberal state was incompatible with liberal justice.

CHAPTER FOUR

Durham and Tocqueville on Religion

Durham was convinced that assimilation was "already commencing" in Lower Canada and that the reforms associated with it would be welcome to the mass of the people.[1] Some aspects of his argument for the inevitability of assimilation have been discussed earlier; we now consider the one that he himself seems to have believed the most important.

As a liberal, Durham took the principle of religious toleration to be the defining characteristic of modern politics. He dated political freedom and religious tolerance both from the Glorious Revolution and the settlement of 1688. He assumed, as we shall see, that the alternation of parties in office – what he refers to in one passage as the merely "ordinary animosities of party in a free country" – is possible only in a tolerant society, that is, only where parties or factions claiming authority to rule on the basis of intransigent doctrines, for example, God's authority, are not allowed.[2]

He could not help but see it as all-important that religious dissensions were almost non-existent in Lower Canada. "It is a subject of very just congratulation," he wrote, "that religious differences have hardly operated as an additional cause of dissension."[3] The French and English might be at war, but they were not quarrelling about Protestantism and Catholicism. In his eyes this fact was the surest sign that the foundation of a modern nation had been laid in Lower Canada. It was evidence that the Roman Catholic church had relinquished its role as support for the laws and institutions of the old French-Canadian way of life and was ready to accept the progressive reforms that he was putting forward. The idea of "virtue," defined by the church, was no longer at the centre of politics.

Nevertheless, it was not part of his program to abolish Catholicism. On the contrary, he proposed measures to support the Roman Catholic endowments in Lower Canada.[4] Durham's complete position on church and state, religion and society, shows two faces perhaps not easily reconciled. He held, in the first place, that authoritative religious demands must be excluded from the political arena. But he argued as well that religious institutions must be maintained and that religious teachers must be encouraged to supply a certain political influence. "Virtue" was to be displaced, but was nevertheless to be allowed, even assisted, to linger on the periphery.

Like other liberals of the time, Durham was involved in the movement to grant relief from political and educational disabilities to English dissenters and Roman Catholics. In 1834, for example, he presented dozens of petitions in Parliament from dissenters, and more than one on behalf of Jews. He supported the founding of the University or Durham because it promised to provide higher education for dissenting Christians.[5] On one occasion at least, he lectured his own constituents in Durham county on religious toleration. A man's religion ought not to be inquired into when his services in office were required, he said. He begged his listeners to remember that the Irish Catholics were not aliens but part of the British Empire, fellow subjects.[6]

In short, he was a reformer in this area as in others. At the same time, he identified these reforms with long-held and long-valued British precepts. It was his view that Britain had been an essentially tolerant nation from 1688, and over and over he argued that he was not introducing new principles, but correcting practices that had failed to measure up to the standards laid down with the Revolution. In the passages on the lack of religious dissensions in Canada, he suggests that in its dealings with French Canada, Britain had always exhibited this typical tolerance. A "degree of practical toleration, known in very few communities," he argues, had existed in the province "from the period of the conquest down to the present time."[7] We are accustomed to think of the home country as lagging behind the colonies in the practice of tolerance: the acts of 1774 and 1791 had given Catholics in Quebec political rights denied British Catholics until 1829. But it is Durham's argument that the ease with which the British adopted the tolerant position in Canada is evidence that, in an important sense, Britain in the eighteenth century already adhered to the principle of tolerance.

Durham pictures the contest between the French regime of 1760 – an "unimproving and repressive despotism" – and the conquering British nation as the meeting of the pre-modern and the modern political worlds. He argues, in effect, that the most important characteristic of the two societies in 1760 was not that one was Catholic and the other Protestant, but that one was a society founded on religion – the regime of "virtue" – and the other was a nation based on tolerance – the regime of "freedom and civilization." When he notes that religion was not an issue in the contest of 1837, he is suggesting that he found the quarrels of French and English in the 1830s in all ways less profound, more amenable to a political reconciliation in which all parties could participate, than the confrontation of 1760 – or the wars of the religious parties in seventeenth-century England. The history of Lower Canada showed the regime of "virtue" subsiding and the principle of toleration triumphing.

He does not mention the fact that the Parti patriote was imbued with anti-clericalism, but he must have taken note. It is the position of the clergy on which he concentrates, however.

He saw it as significant that the priests in the province had backed the British during the Rebellion of 1837. The clergy, he argued, had presented "almost the only semblance of stability and organization, and furnished the only effectual support for civilization and order."[8] He may have been merely acknowledging the assistance of the clergy and prudently soliciting their help in the future. "I know of no parochial clergy in the world," he wrote, "whose practice of all the Christian virtues, and zealous discharge of their clerical duties, is more universally admitted, and has been productive of more beneficial consequences." But it is noteworthy that he extends this praise in the context of his comments on the fact of religious toleration in the province, and it is important that he praises the clergy for upholding "civilization." At a deeper level he is applauding them not so much for supporting Britain as for signifying their acceptance of the modern way of life. He can solicit their help because, as he believes, they have already adopted the principle of religious toleration and approved the modern regime.

It could be argued in the light of the subsequent history of the Catholic church in Quebec that Durham was mistaken about the public stance of the clergy in the 1830s, and that the position of the church was purely pragmatic, indicating no real acceptance of the principles of modernity. It may certainly be true that his discussion indicates more about his own political thought than about the true position of the church. There is evidence, however, that in fact the church was surprisingly moderate in the 1830s, more moderate than it became afterwards.[9] Whatever our conclusion about this matter, it is clear that Durham had decided that the Catholics of Lower Canada in 1837 were amenable to modern doctrines.

His position on Catholics and dissenters in England and his praise of the clergy in Lower Canada shows one face of his teaching – the idea that authoritative religious demands are to be excluded from politics. We should think of this view as expressing the typically liberal distrust of religious institutions that we associate with the demand for the separation of church and state. But as I have suggested, Durham's complete position shows another face, for he argues at the same time that moderate religious teachings have "beneficial consequences."[10] In fact, he maintains that the existence of religious institutions in a modern nation is absolutely necessary, and more than that, that these institutions should be guaranteed financial support by the liberal state. Durham was, indeed, one of those British whigs who argued for the establishment of the Church of England in that country.

In a general statement of his principles, prepared for the British election campaign of 1837, he wrote: "I wish to rally as large a portion of the British people as possible, around the existing institutions of the country – the Throne

– the Lords – Commons and the Established Church. I do not wish to make new institutions, but to preserve and strengthen the old."[11]

"I hold that Church and State, or rather religion and the state, ought to be united," he argued on another occasion. "Every government of every state ought to tender to the community religious instruction ... I do not deny that those who differ from the tenets of that establishment ought to be allowed perfect freedom in the enjoyment of their own doctrines; but what I hold is that the State in the first instance, is bound to furnish instruction to the people."[12]

In the Report he argues that a "wise government," meaning as the context indicates, a government concerned to provide "comfort and prosperity" to the mass of the French Canadians, "would have taken care to aid in every possible way the diffusion of their means of religious instruction."[13] That his argument for establishment has nothing to do with an absolute preference for the Church of England is shown by his recommendation for the support of the Catholic endowments in Lower Canada.[14] He argued, in effect, that the Catholic church in that province be established as the Church of England was in England. It was as appropriate, in his opinion, for Catholic priests to carry out the necessary instruction as any other.

Thus, in his English speeches and in his proposals for British North America both, he subscribes to a twofold formula. Because religion can foment harmful dissensions, all uncompromising religious teachings must be excluded from politics. Nevertheless moderate religious doctrines and moderate institutions are in some sense necessary. Durham does not suggest that the two aspects of his position may be in tension. He assumes that establishment can be reconciled with utter toleration and that the church in Lower Canada had learned the necessary trick of advancing salutary religious precepts without pressing intolerant and intransigent political claims.

On the one hand, this teaching about religion and liberalism is ordinary enough. It is certainly not original. Durham expected his readers to find it familiar, and we may still find it commonplace today, especially when it is stated in a general fashion: religion is salutary; tolerance is good. On the other hand, such a teaching clearly presents difficulties. Beneath the generalities is the suggestion, first, that religion and liberalism are fundamentally opposed, and second, that the wise legislator will find a way of reconciling them. Durham argued that religion may be harmful in a liberal nation, but also that it is beneficial. Certain forms must be prohibited; some forms are absolutely necessary. Although today we may be happy with the idea that religion and liberal institutions should coexist, we may not always be willing to entertain the suggestion that some forms of religious belief may destroy society. And we may be even less willing to consider the idea that without religion our liberal institutions will decline. Consequently, it is worthwhile to recapture Durham's unstated assumptions.

Although Durham's analysis tells us enough to suggest why religion may be harmful, there is little in his work to indicate why it may be necessary. For an argument that acknowledges the two faces of this nineteenth-century position, and then shows us how to think of them together, we must turn to Tocqueville. His conclusions were very like Durham's, but his treatment of the issue is fuller. Tocqueville, no less than Durham, believed that liberal society must be utterly tolerant of diverse sects. He argued forthrightly against the establishment of any sect in the United States, because he held that in that society establishment could not be reconciled with tolerance.[15] But like Durham again, he argued at the same time that some form of religious instruction was required and that it was to be supplied by church bodies.

Tocqueville, indeed, was struck by the religious character of life in the United States; in this modern, liberal, commercial society, the citizens were still ardent church-goers! He noted that Europeans were accustomed to think of religion as the enemy of freedom and progress. The American experience seemed to show, however, that these two "perfectly distinct elements," the spirit of religion and the spirit of freedom, could be "marvellously combined."[16] Durham, describing the "progressive civilization" of the New England states, had noted that every new village had its "schoolhouse and place of public worship," every new city, its "exchanges, courthouses and municipal halls" and "fine churches."[17] He writes as if churches were as typical of the American way of life as institutions of self-government and commerce. For Tocqueville this was something that certainly required explanation. In the introduction to the first volume of *De la Démocratie*, he describes American "civilization" as "le produit ... de deux éléments parfaitement distincts, qui ailleurs se sont fait souvent la guerre, mais qu'on est parvenu, en Amérique, à incorporer en quelque sorte l'un dans l'autre, et à combiner merveilleusement. Je veux parler de l'*esprit de religion* et de l'*esprit de liberté*."[18] He is addressing a European audience in this passage. It is his European readers, especially, as he says, the "partisans de la liberté," who associate religion with the forces of repression. It is his task to assure them that the American example is proof that religion can be freedom's surest friend.

Tocqueville's argument turns on his famous teaching about the mœurs. Religious instruction is to be valued he argues, because it inculcates the mœurs. Advocates of freedom "doivent savoir qu'on ne peut établir le règne de la liberté sans celui des mœurs, ni fonder les mœurs sans les croyances."[19] We might think of the mœurs as those tacit understandings about good and bad, right and wrong, on which (the sociologists tell us) every viable society rests. But it is not Tocqueville's view that the mœurs simply muster consensus on all aspects of society. The mœurs of a free society, he argues, will not license freedoms, but restrict them. American mœurs rendered certain acts virtually unthinkable, and associated others with ideas of disapproval and punishment. That is, they promoted consensus in some areas of human endeavour, chiefly, in Tocqueville's opinion, the areas delineated by the criminal law, while leaving other areas wide open to debate. As a result, the areas open to debate were freer – and the freedom was more secure – than in Europe.

He gives the full argument by way of an analysis of the earliest American Puritan settlements. We do not have to take Tocqueville as an authority on the Puritans, but nothing gives us a better picture of the way in which he thought that religion both constrained and enabled freedom in nineteenth-century America than his discussion of those early communities. In "le monde moral" of Puritan society, he argues, "tout est classé, coordonné, prévu, décidé à l'avance"; in "le monde politique ... tout est agité, contesté, incertain; ... dans l'un, obéissance passive, bien que volontaire; dans l'autre, indépendance, mépris de l'expérience et jalousie de toute autorité."[20]

The supposition is that men cannot legislate for themselves in all areas and hope to remain free. Some actions must be ruled out by dogmatic belief. Americans enjoyed a liberty unknown in Europe because they did not contest all possible public issues.[21] The pattern established in Puritan times, he argues, could still be found in nineteenth-century America. It had been perpetuated by other Protestant sects and by the Catholics. Like Durham, Tocqueville believed that the Catholics of North America, as much as any other sect, had made their peace with liberalism, exchanging claims to participate directly in politics for a subtle, continuing influence in a tolerant society.[22]

Neither writer, I suggest, argues that liberalism and Christianity should be seen as equivalent doctrines. They do not imply, for example, that liberalism is the political expression of Christianity or a development of biblical precepts, nor do they argue that religion simply sanctifies the liberal state, providing support in this way for political obligation. Both associate liberalism with freedom and religion with constraint, docility, and obedience. Religious teachings are required exactly because they do not encapsulate liberal principles, but instil ideas at odds with liberalism. Both would argue that unless the subjects on which men debate and legislate are sharply curtailed by habits and suppositions inculcated by religious dogma, self-government will prove impossible. Tocqueville is explicit. When religious belief fails in America, freedom, too, will fail.

From the arguments of Durham and Tocqueville on liberalism and religion, we must conclude that just as patriotism and love of homeland will persist in the liberal society of the future, so will religious beliefs. But this does not entitle us to argue that "cultural" differences will remain. The society of "freedom and civilization" will be continental and perhaps world-wide. It offers advantages, freedom not the least. But the patriotism it inspires is reflective and well considered; the same must be said of the religions it supports. As Tocqueville argues, exactly because the society is tolerant – meaning that intolerant and intransigent sects and doctrines have been banished – it will exhibit few differences: "Il arrivera donc un temps où l'on pourra voir dans l'Amérique du Nord cent cinquante millions d'hommes ... qui tous appartiendront à la même famille, qui auront le même point de départ ... la même religion ... les mêmes mœurs."[23] If a society is to be free, then "intolerant" religious claims must be suppressed. The mild are necessary; but necessarily they must be mild. We will all have more or less the same religion, as Tocqueville says, and the particularity that depends on religion will be lost.

CHAPTER FIVE

"Responsible Government" and Empire

For most of Durham's commentators – his contemporaries, the Edwardian scholars, and the British and Canadian historians of the twentieth century – "responsible government" is by far the issue of greatest importance in the Report. It is "responsible government" on which the oceans of ink have been spilt and great reputations established.

It has seemed important first because it involved a thoroughgoing reform of government within the colonies. As I suggested in chapter one, "responsible government" has often been taken to have promoted a more democratic form of government for British North America (see the discussion in chapter six). But it has interested commentators chiefly because it was meant, according to Durham's own account, to maintain the colonies' ties with the home country. Durham argued that when the political constitution of the colonies had been reformed, the imperial connection would be more secure. "Responsible government" was a prescription for empire, and as long as interest in the empire and Commonwealth remained high, interest in Durham on "responsible government" flourished.

Chester New saw the Report as "the cornerstone of the first British nation beyond the seas ... the great watershed of British imperial history ... one of the few events of world-history of which one can say that this is the beginning of something absolutely new under the sun."[1] Reginald Coupland writes in the same vein: "The immense historical importance of the Durham Report lies in the fact that it established the principles on which the British Commonwealth of Nations has been built."[2]

What commentators like New and Coupland would like to say is that Durham found the formula that would meet the colonists' desire for self-government while at the same time ensuring a degree of British control – a magic formula for colonial autonomy within the empire. But the commentators have always been sensitive to the difficulties inherent in this idea. In fact, they have been torn between the wish to praise Durham as the architect of the second empire and an underlying suspicion that he was simply confused. It is easy enough to see that the grant of "responsible government" was meant to promote colonial self-government. But just how did Durham mean it to further British interests? What the commentators usually say is that he matched "responsible government" with a second measure, one that was meant exactly to check and limit the effects of "responsible government." This second measure, it is said, was for a more-or-less formal division of powers between Britain and the colonies – Britain was to retain some power to legislate in British North America – and it was by means of this division of powers, the commentators maintain, that Durham meant to tie the colonies to the home country. This idea has attracted all the attention: the view that by first proposing "responsible government," and then limiting it with the recommendation for a division of powers, Durham intended to gratify both colonial and metropolitan ambitions.

But I suggest that the commentators have had the same difficulty with Durham on empire as they have had with the assimilation proposal. To argue that Durham proposed to allow Britain power to interfere directly in colonial affairs supposes that he could tolerate the idea that the colonists should be subjected to political leaders against whom they had no appeal. Why should he, as a mainstream liberal, have found this idea any more appealing than the idea that the English-speaking colonists should dominate the French? There is certainly a puzzle about the passages in the Report on empire. It is not easy to see the grounds on which Durham argued that the empire would be strengthened by his proposals. The fact is – and it is striking, given the commentators' contentions – that Durham says nothing to support the idea that he is proposing a new program for imperial relations, a new law, policy, or scheme of any kind. He notes briefly that some observers had contended that the introduction of "responsible government" would change the status of the colonies within the empire, but he says little to develop this notion. For the most part, he writes blithely as if the old semi-dependent status of the colonies is simply bound to continue after "responsible government." In other words, although there are passages in the Report to suggest that he was prepared to put up with the existing state of affairs, there is nothing to lead us to argue that he himself was ready to prescribe measures to reinforce it.

The commentators, beginning with the idea that he meant the empire to endure, come to conclusions that do not fit with Durham's liberal views. We may get closer to his position on empire if we keep constantly before us his belief that self-government is the proud right of every Englishman (and for that matter, every French Canadian), and attempt to see how he reconciled this belief with colonial status for British North America. To solve the puzzle, let us first look at "responsible government" and then at the passage on empire – in particular the one passage that is usually singled out as supporting the idea of a division of powers.

Durham agreed with reformers in British America that the problem with colonial constitutions had to do with exactly those features that limited self-government. Under the practices that had grown up in the colonies in the years after the Constitution Act of 1791, the representative legislative assemblies were relegated to an advisory role. The executive council in each colony, appointed on the advice of the governor, retained place and power whatever the outcome of the elections and whatever the composition of the assembly.[3] Someone like Lord John Russell could defend this system by arguing that it gave the colonists at least a voice in their own affairs, while ensuring the continuing representation of home-country interests; the assembly represented popular colonial interests, it was said, while the executive, composed of men from that stratum of colonial society that could be depended on to co-operate with the governor and the Colonial Office, represented the empire.

But by the 1830s, objections to the system had risen to fever pitch in the colonies. The reformers claimed that the system perpetuated rule by provincial elites who acted solely for themselves – ignoring the interests of the colonies and the Colonial Office alike. It was certainly true that able and ambitious reformers in the assemblies were seldom appointed to the executive or legislative councils.[4] Many reformers believed that these evils could be remedied by introducing elective executive councils.[5] However, there were others – among them Etienne Parent and Robert Baldwin – who suggested that it would be preferable to follow the practice established in Britain and to nominate the executive council from the majority party in the assembly, or from those acceptable to the majority party.[6] This is the practice that Durham recommends and it is what comes to be know as "responsible government." "It is difficult to conceive what could have been their theory of government" he wrote, "who imagined that in any colony of England a body invested with the name and character of a representative Assembly, could be deprived of any of those powers which, in the opinion of Englishmen, are inherent in a popular legislature."[7] The political executive, he argues, is to carry on "by means of those in whom [the] representative body has confidence," and to forfeit office if it loses the support of the majority in that body "on great questions of policy."[8]

It was Russell's argument that "responsible government" meant abandoning the system that rendered the colonies formally dependent. If the colonial executive could be held to account by the colonial house, he argued, it could not at the same time speak for, and answer to, the Colonial Office and the imperial parliament. "Responsible government," in his opinion was suitable only for completely autonomous nations. To grant it would mean the end of British influence in the colonies forever.[9]

In the face of this view, we have Durham's insistence that the grant of "responsible government" would not weaken but strengthen the British influence. The commentators have found Russell's position easier to understand and some have concluded that Russell was right and Durham wrong.[10] But most have attempted to save Durham's position in some way. The discussion has come to centre on one passage. At a first reading, it does indeed appear to bear out the supposition that Durham proposed to limit the autonomy implied by the grant of "responsible government," by allowing Britain power to continue legislating for the colonies: "The matters which ... concern us are very few. The constitution of the form of government, – the regulation of foreign relations, and of trade with the mother country, the other British colonies and foreign nations, – and the disposal of public lands, are the only points of which the mother country requires a control."[11]

It was C.P. Lucas who first interpreted this passage to mean that Durham proposed something like a division of powers between the colonies and Britain, with the home country retaining the power to legislate in four critical areas: the constitution, foreign relations, trade, and the disposal of new lands in the colonies. Although Durham's wording was clearly intended to leave the impression that home-country interests in colonial affairs were minimal, Lucas maintained that, in fact, Durham had proposed to place substantial restrictions on the colonies. "It will be noted how very limited were the powers which Lord Durham proposed to give to the colonies under responsible government," he wrote.[12] "Responsible government was the dynamic idea in the *Report*," argues Gerald Craig, "but it must not be forgotten how severely the idea was qualified by Lord Durham."[13] Read in this way, the passage added up to a concrete prescription: colonial autonomy in some areas, subordination in others.[14]

However, by the first decade of this century, all could see that the senior dominions had grown markedly independent, and it was difficult not to attribute this growth to "responsible government." Indeed, Lucas argues that Durham had not foreseen that "responsible government" would mean a gradual loosening of ties. In short, Lucas first read the Report as a proposal for a division of powers, and then pointed out that it had been more or less ineffective.[15] It was a strange argument on which to base his picture of Durham as one of the great empire-makers. Nevertheless, he concluded:

And yet it is impossible to study the Report without feeling that such a statement of its limitations does it less than justice. It has been attempted in the foregoing pages to lay stress upon what has been termed Lord Durham's constructiveness. To all times and to all sorts and conditions of men he has preached the doctrine, that for peoples, as for individuals, the one thing worth living for is to make, not to destroy; to build up ... It is as a race of makers that the English will live to all time, and it is as a prophet of a race of makers that Lord Durham lives.[16]

Despite Lucas' qualms about the effectiveness of the proposal, the division-of-powers reading took on an independent life. Lionel Curtis, the prophet of the movement for imperial federalism, argued that the germ for that great project could be detected in Durham's division-of-powers proposal. Like Lucas, Curtis believed that Durham had not foreseen the consequences of "responsible government," but he argued that Durham's scheme could be improved in order to provide a truly sound basis for relations between the metropolis and the colonies. His own formula was meant to retain the spirit of the Report while erecting a stronger edifice. The division of powers was to be extended so that in each nation of the empire, including Britain, internal matters would be the affair of a local parliament, elected by the citizens of the nation, while imperial matters were administered by an imperial parliament, with taxing powers, elected by the citizens of the empire.[17]

Reginald Coupland, writing some years later, took a different tack. He argued that although Durham had proposed a division of powers, he had never intended it to last. It was Coupland's opinion that Durham had meant from the first to foster the growth of independent nations within the imperial framework.[18] This is the basis of his belief that Durham should be hailed as the founder of the Commonwealth.[19]

In *The Durham Report and British Policy*, Ged Martin rings the changes again. He suggests that Durham had proposed a division of powers, and has intented it to be permanent. But he concludes that since it entirely failed – Durham's "formal and mechanical division of powers could not be sustained" – to regard Durham as a prophet, empire-maker, or even as an administrator possessed of ordinary astuteness is the height of absurdity.[20] In this respect, as in others, he argues, the reputation of the Report has been grossly inflated. From Lucas to Martin, then, the division-of-powers reading prevails, interpreted sometimes as a formula for building the empire and sometimes as a formula for dismembering it. All the praise, all the interest centres on this reading. Even Martin, who is so eager to reduce the Report to dust and ashes, relies on the standard approach.

But the division-of-powers reading has more to do with the commentators' hopes and fears for empire and Commonwealth than with the plain sense of the text. We must look at the disputed passage in its entirety. It is worth noting first how Durham prefaces it: "I know that it has been urged ... that a colony which should name all its own administrative functionaries, would, in fact, cease to be dependent." In other words, he introduces Russell's argument. But instead of developing it, Durham goes on immediately to argue that the home country should consider interfering only in matters that affect imperial relations:

The matters which so concern us, are very few. The constitution of the form of government, – the regulation of foreign relations, and of trade with the mother country, the other British Colonies, and foreign nations – and the disposal of the public lands, are the only points of which the mother country requires a control. This control is now sufficiently secured by the authority of the Imperial Legislature; by the protection which the Colony derives from us against foreign enemies; by the beneficial terms which our laws secure to its trade; and by its share of the reciprocal benefits which would be conferred by a wise system of colonization.

The first thing to notice is that Durham assures his readers that he is not proposing anything new. He argues that Britain has a legitimate interest in colonial affairs and should control some colonial matters, but he says that, "this control is now sufficiently secured." He has no new program, law, or policy to put forward. The plain sense of the passage is that after the grant of "responsible government," Britain will find her control as secure as ever.

With the passage in full before us, it can also be seen that it suggests the means by which that control is to be upheld. Elsewhere in the Report, Durham argues that British interests in the colonies cannot be guaranteed by means of military force. To attempt to hold the colonies by armed force will merely precipitate revolution and in that way sever the connection.[21] In the passage we are considering now, he suggests the alternative to armed force, and it turns out to be nothing more formal or rigorous than an appeal to colonial interests. Thus, he argues that imperial control of the form of government in the colonies is guaranteed by the "authority of the imperial legislature"; that is, the colonists will themselves choose to live under the British form of government, after Durham's reforms have been effected, because as all will agree, the British system is unequalled. Similary, British trade interests will be secured by the fact that the colonists desire trade preferences. What will keep the British North Americans steadfast on foreign affairs? What better than the colonists' sense that they need the British army to control American aggression? And finally, the colonists will welcome a program for immigration from Britain and the opening of new lands administered by the home country because they are sensible of the advantages of an orderly extension of the frontier and an increased population. The whole passage, in short, reads not like a list of reasons why Britain must keep the colonies down in order to protect her interests, so much as a list of reasons why the colonies will be eager to promote the imperial connection. As Durham puts it: "A perfect subordination, on the part of the Colony, on these points, is secured by the advantages which it finds in the continuance of its connexion with the Empire."[22] Elsewhere he argues, in the same vein, that "it is not in the terrors of the law ... that the secure and honourable bond of connexion is to be found. It exists in the beneficial operation of ... British institutions ... which, if rightly organized ... would render a change of institutions only an additional evil to the loss of protection and commerce of the British Empire."[23]

Russell argued that "responsible government" would mean colonial independence and spell the end of the empire. I suggest that there is a sense in which Durham comes close to agreeing. He knows as well as Russell that it will sever the colonies' formal, constitutional connection with the metropolis: "I admit that the system which I propose who would, in fact, place the internal government of the colony in the hands of the colonists themselves." "I know that it has been urged ... that a colony which should name all its own administrative functionaries, would, in fact, cease to be dependent."[24] Nevertheless, Durham argues that his proposals will strengthen the empire, and the passages above suggest why. Once the causes of discontent have been removed and the colonists are able to name their own administrative officers, the danger of armed revolt will be obviated and colony and home country will be free to pursue policies that will promote the interests they have in common. The colonies will understand that there is more to be gained from retaining the British name than rejecting it, and it is this perception of mutual advantage that will form the surest tie.[25] The argument suggests, indeed, that it was the scheme favoured by Russell that was the real threat to empire. The irritation of imperial intervention and the limits on self-government under the old system were the factors that wore away colonial loyalty and the colonists' sense of the benefits of connection.

In a series of open letters responding to Russell on "responsible government," Joseph Howe gives a good exposition of this difference between Russell and Durham. Howe objected to Russell's description of the probable consequences of "responsible government" because, as he argued, Russell seemed to assume that the colonies and the home country must always be at odds on the major issues. It was Howe's opinion, and on this ground he supported Durham and the proposal for "responsible government," that on the contrary, the interests of the colonies and the metropolis were compatible, and that amiable relations would follow once the colonists' irritations had been removed. He captures Durham's views exactly. With "responsible government" all attempts to break the ties would cease.[26] I argued in chapter three that Durham maintains that the colonists' pride and affection for Britain and the empire will blossom with freedom and prosperity. Thus, while he speaks of Britain's "control" and the colonies' "subordination," it is not armed force and not even law that are to enforce the control and subordination, but mutual advantage and commercial interest. Mutual advantage and interest: this is to be the cement of the imperial connection, and not a "formal and mechanical division of powers." In the commission that Durham drew up appointing Charles Buller to investigate land use in the colonies, for example, he speaks of an "intimate" and "permanent" connexion between Britain and her colonial empire ... founded on common interests and productive ... advantage."[27] Patriotism and loyalty depend on prosperity; prosperity depends on political institutions enabling self-government – on these tenets hang Durham's formula for imperial relations.

Did he believe that advantage and interest would suffice? Was he merely seeking to cloak a proposal for political autonomy acceptably when he used terms like "intimate" and "permanent"? Was he, in fact, proposing complete political independence for the colonies? It was certainly Edward Gibbon Wakefield's opinion that the colonies would acquire the powers of completely independent nations in time, while continuing to remain British in name, and he associates this idea with the Durham Report.[28] On this ground, we might say that were Durham here today he would express satisfaction with the progress of Her Majesty's Canadian subjects and see it as the fulfilment of his hopes of 1839.

It is impossible to suppose that Durham could wholeheartedly approve of a formal scheme for British intervention in the colonies. He may have been prepared to tolerate the existing situation, but he did not intend to bolster imperial powers in the colonies, or to "institutionalize" them with a proposal for a division of powers. Such a reading of the Report is simply incompatible with his political philosophy. Lucas's hopes for a program of imperial relations that would allow Britain to retain political rights in the dependencies are in line with his own willingness to accept a degree of permanent subordination for the French Canadians. Lucas does not find breaches of the principle of equal opportunity entirely offensive. For Durham however, equality, freedom and self-government cannot be compromised. No citizens, not the British North Americans, not the French in Lower Canada, should be subjected to legislative decisions by rulers against whom they do not have formal political rights, that is, rulers that they cannot hope to remove from power. This is the cornerstone of his thought on political constitutions and nationality alike. The French must not be subject to English rule; the mass of the populace represented in the legislative assembly must not be subject to political elites against whom they have no appeal; the colonists should not be subject to the government of a foreign country. But the commentators who have missed Durham's thought on nationality and suppose that he meant the English in Canada to continue dominating the French have similarly missed his position on empire.

Coupland and others suggest that it is difficult to reconcile Durham's recommendations for the assimilation of the French with his history of sympathy for the rebellions of the small and subject nationalities of Europe following the defeat of Napoleon and the Congress of Vienna. Coupland argues that the assimilation proposal was one "that in other circumstances he would seem the least likely man to make."[29] Durham could make a case for the freedom of the Norwegians, the Poles, and the Belgians, he notes, but he was unable to see the merits of the French-Canadian cause. However, a review of Durham's statements shows that he treated the European rebellions not as attempts to establish boundaries defining nations of distinct language and "manners," but as movements to overthrow tyranny and to found liberal political institutions.

His maiden speech in the House of Commons was a plea for intervention on behalf of the people of Norway in their bid for independence from Sweden. He declared his support for the "spirit of national independence" evidenced by the Norwegians, and predicted that this "invincible" spirit would "extend through every part of Europe."[30] At a time when the right of the French people to form their own constitution had been recognized by the allied powers, he said, the nation of Norway should not be compelled to bow beneath a foreign yoke. He repeatedly denounced "the club of confederated monarchs at Vienna, who appeared to have met, not to watch over the interests of Europe, but as contemners of public faith and justice, as the spoilators of Saxony and the oppressors of Norway."[31] He accused Castlereagh of executing the spoilation and partition of whole countries. In a passage that lends perhaps some credence to Coupland's contention, he argued that Castlereagh had divided populations possessing the same "manners," language, and customs. But in all, Durham's emphasis is on what he sees as the fact that these small nationalities were delivered into bondage. It was his opinion, he said, that Castlereagh had separated subjects from monarchs they respected while handing over independent states to sovereigns whose rule had been immemorially the object of their detestation; Castlereagh had assisted tyrants and upheld European despotism.[32] Like others in the Grey ministry in the early 1830s, Durham worked hard to secure Belgian independence, and in those years, too, his name was linked with the cause of the Polish revolutionaries, (see chapter three), not so much because he spoke out on this subject as because he had by that time established the kind of reputation that would lead English writers to suppose that he would denounce the Russian incursion as a matter of course.[33]

What Durham supported in the European rebellions was not nationalism as such, but the freedom of subject peoples to assert themselves against autocratic rule in order to bring in a liberal regime. "The first and most important reason why nations had to become states," says Charles Taylor, speaking of exactly those early nineteenth-century struggles, "is that it was seen as a condition of self-rule."[34] This is Durham's view exactly. In his analysis, the French Canadians could not be given the sympathy due the Norwegians, Poles, and Belgians because they were advocating conservative measures in opposition to liberal hopes.

The Edwardian dream of "Great Britain, Greater Britain, Greatest Britain," and the later hopes for the Commonwealth, endowed "responsible government" with a tremendous sense of importance only tenuously connected with the substance of the Report and Durham's analysis of problems in British North America.[35] Much of that aura remains. By the 1960s, it is true, attitudes towards the empire had changed. Burroughs argues in a review of the 1969 edition of New's biography that "our sober detached appraisal of Durham's career has little in common with the emotional, patriotic involvement evinced by writers of a former generation when the British empire was in its heyday."[36]

But it is only the adjectives that have changed. The analysis of the Report given its stamp by the turn-of-the-century writers is still with us. "Responsible government" retains its peculiar prominence and the division-of-powers reading is standard. As a result, Durham's political program and the relationship of the assimilition proposal and "responsible government" have remained obscure. Heavy-handed judgments about the assimilation proposal are still the order of the day, while Durham's mainstream thought remains unexplored.

CHAPTER SIX

"Responsible Government" in the Colonies

With the introduction of "responsible government," the political executive was to answer to the legislative assembly, meaning that it would be chosen from those acceptable to the majority in the assembly, and could be dismissed on "great questions of policy" by a majority vote. In external affairs, the introduction of "responsible government" rendered the colonies more independent. In domestic politics it spelled the end of the "family compacts," the political cliques in each province.[1]

From this broad description it would be easy to conclude that Durham saw "responsible government" as having a democratic thrust, and some commentators have seen it this way. However, Durham usually writes as if "responsible government" were a way of restraining democratic demands. He describes it as a measure that will strengthen the political executive so as to enable it to "limit" or "balance" the popular house. It is true that he regarded "responsible government" as valuable because it would be the means, on occasion, by which leaders betraying popular interests could be removed from office. But he seems to have supposed that it would usually work to maintain the executive in office so that it in fact became less responsive to immediate popular demands. In short, although he may appear at first sight to be simply promoting democracy, a closer look suggests that it might be truer to argue that he was something of an anti-democrat – if that label is not a misnomer for someone who so clearly had popular interests at heart.

In one passage, for example, Durham speaks of the need for a "limitation on the present powers of the representative bodies" in the colonies.[2] In another he refers to the "true principle of limiting popular power."[3] He argues that the Assembly of Lower Canada had "endeavoured to extend its authority in modes totally incompatible with the principles of constitutional liberty," that it had "transgressed our notions of the proper limits of Parliamentary interference."[4] In the same vein he suggests that what was needed in Upper Canada was "an executive sufficiently powerful to curb popular excesses."[5] Whatever he intended by "responsible government," it was no mere strengthening of the powers of the popular house.

Behind this seemingly anti-democratic thrust of his thought lies a long tradition in British liberalism. Throughout the eighteenth century and well into the nineteenth, British political thinkers, both whig and tory, held forth on the dangers of "popular power." They argued that a strong political executive relatively immune to popular demand, and an appointed upper legislative chamber, were as necessary to good government as a popularly elected assembly. The good political constitution must comprise a "monarchic" branch (the cabinet, the ministers of the Crown), and an "aristocratic" branch (the upper legislative house), as well as a "democratic" branch. This was the famous "balanced" or mixed constitution.

During the Great Reform Bill debates of 1830–1, for example, both whigs and tories argued that mixed government, "balance," was their object. Grey, for the whigs, maintained that the popular branch of government needed bolstering in the face of trends that had long favoured the aggrandizement of the executive. He suggested that the balanced constitution established with the Glorious Revolution of 1688 had lost its harmonious proportions over the years, and insisted that the reforms put forward by his party would do no more than restore to the popular house powers it had once possessed. The bill, he said on one occasion, would "support the interests of the Crown, the Aristocracy and the people," and in this way uphold the constitution on which Britain's prosperity had so long depended.[6] Peel, for the tories, argued that, on the contrary, the reforms would have the effect of destroying the "balance" of 1688 by securing the permanent ascendency of the popular house. It would "convert the mixed government under which we had lived into a simple democracy."[7] Grey had long supported parliamentary reform; Peel had long opposed it. But to judge from his argument, Grey no more than Peel wished to open the door to democracy.[8]

Durham's position on the Reform Bill was much like Grey's. He, too, claimed to be upholding the constitution of 1688 by means of measures that would restore the "balance." In his first speech on the bill he argued that "we have not introduced anything new or unknown to our Constitution." To give "security to the three estates is the object of our bill," he said.[9] Indeed, he argued for mixed government throughout his career in England, and he apparently saw no reason why the colonies of British North America should have anything less than this best constitution.

It seemed to some observers at this time that with the July Revolution in France, the Reform Bill in England, and Jackson's election in the United States, "the three leading countries of the West had announced their entry upon the Democratic Era."[10] The Philosophical Radical party in Britain, for example, was convinced that the most progressive and democratic doctrines would be given concrete form in British North America after the rebellions.

But there is no enthusiasm for new doctrines, certainly no enthusiasm for the Radicals' view of democracy, in the Report. Durham describes the constitutional reforms he proposed for the colonies as the expression of the principles of 1688.[11] "It needs no change in the principles of government," he argued, "no invention of a new constitutional theory, to supply the remedy which would, in my opinion, completely remove the existing political disorders."[12] He apparently hoped to persuade the colonists and assure his whig colleagues that the tried and true British formula was more appropriate for British North America than the new democratic schemes of the Radicals.

It might be argued that this was a futile appeal to the past and, therefore, doomed. Nevertheless, in the first place, although Canada has undoubtedly become more democratic in some respects since Durham's period – the franchise is broader and mass parties have grown up – that strong relatively independent executive that he believed so necessary is still a feature of British parliamentary systems today. It is still true to say that Canada's constitution exhibits the "balance" of which he approved.[13] Second, we shall see that Durham's fear of democratic excesses is not grounded on a distrust of the "people" as such. He does not mean to defend elite interests – the privileges and property of the upper classes – against the demands of the mass of the people. Indeed, British advocates of mixed government from the eighteenth century on argued that their constitutional measures would benefit the "people" and work to further popular interests better than "simple" democracy. In Durham's case, at least, we must take this claim seriously. It is impossible to believe that he meant to benefit the colonial elites at the expense of the populace at large. When he speaks in the Report of "order, tranquillity and improvement" as the goals of good government, it is clearly the settler population of the colonies that he hopes to benefit, the mass of the people, and not the office holders and the governing clique. We have seen that he suggests the introduction of his reforms as the way to bring to British North America a prosperity comparable to New England's, and nothing in his picture of life in New England suggests that he admired it because it promoted wealth for a minority.

Durham argued that freedom for the "people" was the great benefit of the mixed constitution: "I hold that in our form of government by King, Lords and Commons, there will be found as great a degree of liberty as ever existed in any other country of the world, and as much rational liberty as any people under the sun can, or ought to, enjoy."[14] He suggests that the balanced constitution will provide a surer guarantee than simple democracy that there will be any freedom at all in the long run. In line with this, as we have seen, he described the transgressions of the popular house in Lower Canada as a threat to "constitutional liberty."

His fears are not grounded on a distrust of the "people" but on a distrust of political leaders who claim to speak for popular interests. Everything he writes is marked by a typically whiggish distrust of political leaders and a typical attention to the corrupting effects of political power. But it must be said that he perhaps especially distrusts popular leaders. At bottom, I suggest, the argument for a "balanced" or mixed form of government as Durham expounds it, is an argument against democratic tyranny. What the whigs and tories of his day meant by "simple" democracy was what we now call democratic or popular tyranny. Durham's proposals for the reform of the colonial constitutions are intended to build safeguards against the emergence of a form of government in which rulers use their claim to represent popular interests in order to exploit the populace, and in which the people are so closely tied to their leaders that they are unable to depose them.

He believes, in line with traditional thought on the mixed regime, that a salutary "balance" of more democratic and less democratic institutions is the remedy. He argues that to prevent democratic tyranny some government institutions must be representative and responsive to popular demand, but also – paradoxical as it may seem – that other institutions must be less democratic, that is, less representative and responsive. He meant "responsible government" as a feature of a constitution that would further popular interests, freedom, and prosperity by safeguarding the populace from exploitive popular leaders.

The prospect of popular tyranny haunts his analysis of the "contest of races." He came to the conclusion that the appeal to nationality would sometimes – perhaps always – be the means to reinforce the trend to democratic tyranny. In his analysis, the patriotes were evoking the sentiments of "race" in order to secure their position with an electorate whose political and economic demands they could not meet. The appeal to nationality bound the people to the party, freeing party leaders to pursue goals at odds with popular claims. As we shall see in this chapter and the next, Durham's analysis of the "contest" between French and English and his proposals for union and "responsible government" all turn on this point.

The most ardent advocates of democracy in Britain in the 1830s were the Philosophical Radicals, disciples of Jeremy Bentham and James Mill. They were one of several radical parties in British politics in these years, the most interesting from our perspective because they were democrats, and because they championed Canadian causes. It was as democrats that they mounted a determined opposition to whig policies in British North America and argued for the rebel cause in 1837 and 1838. The presence of an ambitious popular party in the Assembly of Lower Canada, a party claiming the right to govern without restraint from the upper house or executive, seemed to Durham to be a disorder requiring remedy. But in Radical eyes it was cause for rejoicing. The Radicals hoped to see a new democratic order dawn in the New World, and believed that Papineau's party was the herald.[15]

Among the outstanding parliamentary Radicals were Joseph Hume, George Grote, John Temple Leader, Charles Buller, and John Arthur Roebuck. In the extra-parliamentary arena they were supported by journalistic efforts of John Stuart Mill and the organizing abilities of Joseph Parkes, Harriet Grote, and Francis Place.

Durham was well acquainted with their position.[16] He selected as his aides on the Canada mission Charles Buller and Edward Gibbon Wakefield, both identified with the Radicals, and he was careful to consult John Arthur Roebuck, the chief Radical spokesman on Canada, before he left England.[17] He is known to have presented Roebuck's position to Canadian figures during his period in office, presumably in order to determine their reaction.[18] Much of the argument in the Report is addressed to the Radicals and is meant to refute their claims.

Bentham had argued that "Tories and Whigs – both parties ... will be seen to possess the same separate and sinister interest: an interest completely and unchangeably opposite to that of the whole uncorrupt portion of the people."[19] According to Mill, political men were of two sorts, *ceux qui pillent,* and *ceux qui sont pillés.* To take away the power "by which the class *qui pillent* succeed in carrying on their vocation has ever been the problem of government," he wrote.[20] The Radicals, as disciples of Bentham and Mill, dreamed of establishing a party "of the people" in Britain, that is, a party to represent the majority and to govern in their name.[21] The people of England, argued Buller in a pamphlet of 1831, have realized that the governing "oligarchy is swayed by interests distinct from those of the people and incompatible with them ... the happiness of the many is sacrificed to that of the few."[22] The demands of the people, he goes on, must be wrested from unwilling rulers by revolution.

For the old idea of "balance," the Radicals had nothing but scorn. "Talk of balance," Bentham had written, "never will it do: leave that to Mother Goose and Mother Blackstone ... when forces *balance* each other the machine is at a stand."[23] In the "Essay on Government," James Mill attacked the doctrine as "wild, visionary, chimerical." "If there are three powers," he asked, "how is it possible to prevent two of them from combining to swallow up the third?"[24] Bentham's and Mill's disciples treated appeals to "balance" as malicious lies designed to blind the mass of the people to the machinations of the aristocratic/oligarchic whig and tory minority. They saw no value in an independent upper house and perhaps less in a strong political executive; the executive in their view should be no more than a tool of the popular house.[25]

The rise of strong majority parties in the British North American colonies seemed to the Radicals to be an illustration, perhaps a proof, of Benthamite principles. Henry Samuel Chapman argued, after the Parti patriote victory at the polls in 1834, that the idea of "balance" had been discredited in the colonies forever. The people of Lower Canada, he said, had come to see the great value of the "philosophers'" doctrine.[26] Roebuck argued over and over that the patriotes, like the Radicals, represented the great principle of democracy, while the English-speaking "official party" in the executive and legislative councils of Lower Canada, like the British whigs and tories, represented aristocracy, the "sinister" minority interest. The "official party," he said, was a small body of persons who "desire to rule over their fellows without responsibility ... seeking to domineer by force or by fraud over the suffering majority."[27] In his black and white version of utilitarian teachings, all politics was a struggle between the forces of Aristocracy and the forces of Democracy.[28]

The Radical position on Canada was very much the stronger in the British Parliament because it could claim to represent the interests of the Parti patriote in an official capacity. In 1835 Roebuck was commissioned by the Legislative Assembly of Lower Canada to speak for the patriote cause in the British Commons. He orchestrated the Radical attack on the government's policies on Canada in the House until he lost his seat in the 1837 election. After that he continued "out of doors," lobbying, publishing, and speaking at public meetings, always representing the Canadians as blameless and the whigs as villains. When news of the rebellion in Canada reached England late in 1837, he redoubled his efforts.[29] He was a not inconsiderable force in English politics at this time, and to a large extent the status and impact of the Radical party as a whole was tied up with his role as spokesman for the disaffected colonists.[30]

The Radicals endorsed the patriotes not because they were French but because they were the majority party. They believed that Papineau was entitled to take over the government of the province because they were convinced that the patriotes as the majority party – the party "of the people" – represented the colonists of both national origins.[31] "My whole case rested on democracy," Roebuck argued: "The people whom I was representing are democrats."[32]

The appeal of the Radical program cannot be denied; it was, for the New World, a new political doctrine. British North America was to adopt a constitution that the home country would later imitate. It is against this project, apparently so much in tune with the spirit of the age, that Durham chooses to advance old arguments for the old constitution.

In the British parliamentary debates on the Canada question, the Radicals pointed to the fact that some – or as they usually argued, many – individuals of British and of American descent were to be found on the so-called French side of the quarrel. This above all was their proof that it was a quarrel between the majority representing both French-speaking and English-speaking Canadians, and a "sinister," "official" minority. Despite the presence of French and English in Lower Canada, argued Leader on one occasion, the dispute could not be called a "contest of races." It was a conflict between the "people" and a "nominated council": "It was a contest between an oligarchy and the democracy, insulted and trampled down by a miserable minority – an oligarchy who had so long tyrannized over the rest of the community that they think they are deprived of their rights when affairs are ... placed on a proper footing."[33]

By the "nominated council" in this instance, Leader meant the legislative council of the colony – the upper legislative house. The legislative council in each colony was perhaps the chief object of Radical ire. The Radicals charged the councils with frustrating progressive legislation, that is, the measures initiated by the people's representatives in the assemblies. They argued that in Lower Canada the reform of the laws of land tenure and proposals to fund schools and provide for famine relief had all suffered defeat because of the machinations of the legislative council.[34] The legislative council of Lower Canada "represents noboby," argued J.S. Mill, "not the colony, for that is represented in the House of Assembly; not the aristocracy of the colony, for there is no such thing, not the mother country, for that is represented by the Governor and the Executive Council."[35] In a prudent mood, the Radicals would demand an elective legislative council; at other times they called for abolition.[36]

Their position with respect to the executive council was not clear-cut. However, they were not blind to the fact that members of the same circle of family and friends in each province occupied positions in the executive councils as well.[37] At times the Radicals urged elective executive as well as legislative councils. But any measure that would secure the ascendency of the popular house received their approval.[38] It was their aim to aggrandize the powers of the assembly so as to enable the people's representatives to govern in the name of the people. Believing that all the ills of the colonies were the work of the "sinister" minority in the legislative and executive councils, they advanced reforms that seemed designed to neuter or weaken the powers of those institutions.

Durham, viewing the same disorders – the assemblies warring with the councils, the political and economic affairs of the colonies neglected – produced a sharply different analysis. He concluded that the executive and legislative councils of Lower Canada were too weak. He noted first that the legislative assembly of the lower province had gained a surprising control over public moneys. He argued that the patriotes had been able to entertain the idea of running their own administrative program, and for a short time at any rate, had been able to pay their own administrative officers.[39] In other words, they had acted as a self-contained democratic government, effecting public business in the name of the people.

He pointed out that by means of impeachments and committees of inquiry, the assembly had attempted to discredit members of the executive council. Indeed, an outright assault on the upper legislative house had been made by the assembly through an attempt to repeal the points of the Act of 1791 establishing and defining the legislative council. In general, he argued, powers proper to the assembly, such as the power to make a general refusal of supplies – the *ultima ratio* of representative power, as he called it – had been used in an intemperate and destructive manner.[40]

The assembly, in short, had, "endeavoured to extend its authority in modes totally incompatible with the principles of constitutional liberty"; it had "transgressed our notions of the proper limits of Parliamentary interference." Faithful to the idea of "balance," he argued that the executive should be strengthened and the legislature curbed:

The defective system of administration in Lower Canada, commences at the very source of power; and the efficiency of the public service is impaired throughout, by the entire want in the Colony of any vigorous administration of the prerogative of the Crown. The fact is, that, according to the present system, there is no real representative of the Crown in the Province; there is in it, literally, no power which originates and conducts the executive government.

He did not believe that the executive was entirely without resources. He could see as clearly as the Radicals that a small body of men in each province had monopolized government offices and used their positions to further their own interests.[42] "Fortified by family connexion, and the common interest felt by all who held, and all who desired, subordinate office," the executive council was only too able to gratify the interests of individuals and party.[43] But it was nevertheless without the power to meet popular demand or govern the province. "I would not impair a single prerogative of the Crown," he argued; "on the contrary, I believe that the interests of the people of these colonies require the protection of prerogatives which have not hitherto been exercised."[44]

Durham proposed as means to strengthen the executive, two constitutional principles not in operation in the colonies at the time. Both, he argued, had been established in Britain from 1688. The first we may call the money-bill principle. In the constitution he proposed for the united Canadas, money bills were to originate with the executive council. The executive would thus initiate the major legislative programs, and the assembly be confined to review of government budgets and spending.[45] The money-bill principle would have had the effect of furthering the strength, even the independence of the executive, while at the same time endowing the popular house with the power to curb executive excesses.

The second principle was "responsible government." The governor and his executive council were to carry on government "by means of those in whom [the] representative body has confidence," and to resign on an adverse majority vote in the house.[46] Gerald Craig refers to "responsible government" as the "heart of Lord Durham's recommendations, and the reason for the enduring value of his *Report*."[47] William Ormsby speaks of Durham's "two major recommendations," and of the "two great questions of the period": "responsible government and assimilation."[48] The money-bill measure has received little attention. And too often "responsible government" is interpreted as if with this measure Durham hoped to see the executive subordinated and the legislative assembly endowed with the power to make and unmake governments easily.

If we take seriously Durham's own claim to be proposing a measure known in England from 1688, we must suppose that he had in mind the strong, relatively independent political executive. Political scientists and historians usually stress the differences between the British constitution of the eighteenth and nineteenth centuries and the system as it is today.[49] Nevertheless, if we concentrate on relations between the executive and the legislature rather than, for example, the extent of the franchise or party organization, there are noticeable similarities. British ministers in the eighteenth century relied on bribes of "place" and pension to organize and control their support in the lower house; today's ministers rely on the partisan spirit and the promise of advancement within the party, but the strong executive is just as much a fact.[50] Durham meant to introduce a system in which for the most part the executive is supported in office by the majority party in the legislature. "Since the Revolution of 1688," he argued, "the stability of the English constitution has been secured by that wise principle of our Government which has vested the direction of the national policy, and the distribution of patronage in the leaders of the Parliamentary majority."[51]

I do not wish to suggest that Durham wanted to deprive the popular house of the powers that we associate with it today. On the contrary, he regarded the power to review expenditures, and, under "responsible government," to dismiss an executive administering funds in an unsatisfactory fashion, as "inherent" powers of the popular house: "It is difficult to conceive what could have been their theory of government who imagined that in any colony of England a body invested with the name and character of a representative Assembly, could be deprived of any of the powers which, in the opinion of Englishmen, are inherent in a popular legislature."[52] He argues, in fact, that the assembly's "transgressions" had been due in large part to the fact that the inherent powers had been denied it. The assembly had reached for improper powers in an attempt to secure proper ones.[53] In the end, Durham defines the powers appropriate to each branch; he makes what might be called a separation of powers, so that transgressions will cease:

There can be no reason for apprehending that either party would enter on a contest, when each would find its interest in the maintenance of harmony; and the abuse of the powers which each would constitutionally possess, would cease when the struggle for larger powers became unnecessary. Nor can I conceive that it would be found impossible or difficult to conduct a Colonial Government with precisely that limitation of the respective powers which has been so long and so easily maintained in Great Britain.[54]

Just as with the money-bill principle, "responsible government" was to provide the popular house with the power to curb unduly ambitious executives; the system was to "bring the influence of a vigorous public opinion to bear on every detail of public affairs."[55] But the thrust of the proposal, especially in the case of Lower Canada, was meant to effect a "limitation on the present powers of the representative bodies."[56] The assembly was not to be the seat of government. It was to have the power to "balance" the executive, but not the power to govern.

In his analysis of the affairs of Upper Canada, we see Durham applying the doctrine to rather different circumstances. In Upper Canada the executive had retained control of public moneys, and for this reason had been able to undertake "great works ... on an extended scale." Durham greatly admired the energy with which the upper province had tackled the "war on the wilderness" and begun the many great projects he believed were necessary in a new land.[57] It was precisely what Lower Canada, lacking "vigorous administration of the prerogative of the Crown," had been unable to carry out. However, he argues that these works were executed in a spirit of "carelessness and profusion."[58] Just as in Lower Canada, in fact, the executive, unhampered by the restraints traditionally provided by the popular house, had set out to provide patronage for party, family, and friends. But having more money, they were able to do themselves more good. The tory party of Upper Canada flourished mightily, and the economy of the province declined to a corresponding degree.

Moreover, although the assembly was a weak affair, compared to the Lower Canada body, it was, nevertheless (just as in Lower Canada), without the "balance" of the executive, and for that reason it exhibited problems evident in the lower province, if to a lesser extent: "Members of the House of Assembly came to the meeting of the legislature ignorant of the real character of the general interests entrusted to their guardianship, intent only on promoting sectional objects."[59] Even in the case of Upper Canada, then, Durham called for "an executive sufficiently powerful to curb popular excesses." He suggests the remedy in politic form, attributing to the Upper Canadians themselves a desire for institutions that will provide "an executive sufficently powerful" and that, at the same time, will give the majority of the people "some substantial control over the administration of affairs."[60]

In Britain, Durham had campaigned repeatedly for the extension of the franchise; he could only approve the "almost universal suffrage" and the largely fair electoral practices he found in Lower Canada. The claim of the patriotes to govern was based on solid electoral success; they were assuredly the majority party. Durham knew that as well as the Radicals. He also argued that the patriotes shared a "remarkable ... community of interests" with their French-speaking electorate. The members of the learned professions, he noted, were drawn from habitant families and very often remained in the villages in which they had been born, sharing the way of life of the "illiterate habitans." "They are connected with them by all the associations of early youth ... The most uninstructed population anywhere trusted with political power, is thus placed in the hands of a small body of instructed persons, in whom it reposes the confidence which nothing but such domestic connexion, and such community of interest could generate."[61]

But it is exactly this circumstance that he finds alarming. He does not believe that universal suffrage, fair electoral practices, or even a shared "community of interest" are a sufficient guarantee of government responsiveness. Much of his analysis of the political problems of Lower Canada is devoted to showing how, as the years passed, the assembly party had come more and more to pursue its own narrow purposes and to neglect public demand.[62] Indeed, he suggests that it was precisely because the electorate had come to see the patriotes as the only party capable of sharing their interests that the party could ignore the growing economic distress of the province. It had little need to gratify popular demand in order to secure re-election. And this was the road to democratic tyranny.

In his analysis, then, something more than a broad suffrage and community of interest is required for government in the interest of the populace at large. What Durham prescribed was the executive "sufficiently powerful" to curb popular excesses.

As for the legislative councils, so abhorred by the Radicals, he proposed to leave them with much the same powers. Although he remarks on their relative inefficiency – the legislative councils, he argues, had been "little calculated to answer the purpose of placing the effective check which I consider necessary on the popular branch of the legislature" – he suggests that the council in Lower Canada had been able to perform at least some of the necessary functions: "The Colony has reason to congratulate itself on the existence of an institution which possessed and used the power of stopping a course of legislation that, if successful, would have sacrificed every British interest, and overthrown every guarantee of order and national liberty."[63]

In his proposal to establish a legislative council in the united provinces, Durham pointed out that the council could not have the complete powers of the British House of Lords since the authority of the latter rested in part on tradition and social rank, while the members of the colonial house would not be distinguished by birth or hereditary property. But he could not take the absence of an upper class in British North America as sufficient reason to suppose that a nominated upper house would not in some way further good government.

Power to the people's assembly – this was the Radical doctrine. A stronger executive, an effective, nominated upper house – these were Durham's remedies. He did not argue that the popularly elected house was unimportant in "balanced" government. But he insisted that government by elected representatives would not in itself guarantee the popular interest. For Britain and for the New World, the best guarantee of good government was to be found in the old formula for mixed or "balanced" government.

In the years after the publication of the Report and Durham's death (in 1840), the Radicals Charles Buller and Edward Gibbon Wakefield appropriated and popularized the term "responsible government." But although they associated it with Durham's name, they used it to refer to a form of government in which the popular house is dominant and the executive subordinate. In a pamphlet published in 1840, *Responsible Government for the Colonies,* Buller argues that "responsible government" is the foundation of a popular, majoritarian system. "Popular representatives ... are elected as the organs of the people for the purpose of rendering the whole of government constantly agreeable to the people." As a consequence, he goes on, the people's representatives must have "in their own hands control over their own Executive."[64] He refers to both the constitutional principle and the form of government he describes as "responsible government."

In a series of articles from 1844, written (like *Responsible Government*) in terms of Canadian politics, Wakefield singles out as the chief principles of the best constitution, "responsible government," and "ministerial responsibility."[65] The executive, he argues, is to answer to the people's representatives ("responsible government") for the actions of the administrative officers of government ("ministerial responsibility"). He admits that British politics in the 1840s still has the appearance of an older form of government, by which he means the mixed constitution. But he believed that the new, popular form was already emerging. The practical ascendency of the House of Commons is already evident to the perceptive, he argues, although "masked and guarded" so as to seem compatible with the safety of the throne and the House of Lords. "To all practical intents, the House of Commons, though in theory but the third estate of the realm, has become the representative embodiment of the nation as a whole."[66]

Buller tells us that he is writing to "elucidate and apply a doctrine of Lord Durham's Report."[67] Wakefield places a long quotation from the Report at the head of his first article and claims to be following Durham's example in searching out the principles of the British constitution as they apply to the colonies.[68] Both admired Durham. But both used his name to lend credence to Radical hopes and doctrines, and proved to be misleading first interpreters of his position.

The eighteenth-century thinkers argued that the mixed regime, composed of monarchic, aristocratic, and democratic elements, was superior to simple monarchy, aristocracy, and democracy.[69] The classic statement on the subject for most nineteenth-century figures was made by Blackstone. Durham acknowledged Blackstone's influence in his first reform speech in Parliament.[70] According to Blackstone, the great virtue of the balanced constitution is that it transforms petty demands into political programs in the national interest. He argues that ministers of the Crown – the monarchic branch – will inevitably strive to aggrandize offices and careers; the aristocracy in the upper house will seek rewards for class, family, and faction; and members of the Commons will put forward diverse competing claims on behalf of individuals, groups, and localities. But under the operation of the balanced constitution, the Commons vetoes measures designed to benefit only family and faction, while the Lords and Crown reject measures too petty to reconcile with great aims, and the two legislative houses together combine to prune executive power and curb the ambitions of individual ministers.[71] Thus cabinet ministers, members of the Lords, and representatives of particular loyalties and groups find that they can gratify their interests only in terms of programs benefiting many or all: from the lowest political motives, legislation compatible with high principles; and from the selfish schemes of short-sighted men, programs of a kind that the wise and selfless man could approve.

In his English campaigns, Durham argued only for measures to strengthen the popular branch of government. Like Grey, he suggested that under long years of tory government, executive powers had been so swollen as to be intolerable. It was necessary to strengthen the popular element by restoring traditional powers. He urged household suffrage, redistricting, and frequent parliaments – describing all as having once characterized British politics.[72] Even the secret ballot, a measure he adopted only after 1832, was justified in much the same terms: it would be an innovation, but appropriate because it would help to restore the traditional strength of the House of Commons.[73]

In Britain he plumped for a stronger democratic element; in Canada, for a stronger executive. In each case, in Canada as in Britain, his object was the same – redressing the balance. No one branch of government must dominate, no branch become too weak. What he proposed for the Canadas as for Britain was the old constitution of 1688. If different remedies were required, it was because the disorders differed. In Britain, as he saw it, the democratic branch was too weak; in Lower Canada, it was too strong. Durham's argument for a strong executive in Canada is surely the more interesting because he worked so long and so hard in England for a more democratic representation in a stronger House of Commons.

In 1834, on a speaking tour of Scotland and the north of England, he declared his principles in these words: "I have never yet, nor ever will, conceal my sentiments, whether addressing Radicals on the one hand, or Tories on the other. I have ever stated and avowed what my principles are. I hold that in our form of government by King, Lords and Commons, there will be found as great a degree of liberty as ever existed in any other country of the world."[74] During the election campaign of 1837, he reiterated the position:

I wish to rally as large a portion of the British people as possible around the existing institutions of the country – the Throne – the Lords – Commons and the Established Church. I do not wish to make new institutions but to preserve and strengthen the old ... It has been my ruling principle throughout my political life to endeavour to bring all classes, especially the middle and lower, within the pale of the true, not the spurious constitution ... to make them feel that whilst the Crown enjoyed its prerogatives, and the upper classes their honours, they were also invested with privileges most valuable to them, and, moreover, that all, separately and collectively, rested on the common basis of national utility.[75]

He had first put forward these views in the House of Commons in 1821, arguing that because the majority of the representatives in the House had been returned by improper influence – the influence of the Crown in some instances, the influence of the aristocracy in others – the House had come to possess interests distinct from those of the people: "I contend therefore that it is the paramount duty of every true lover of his country to endeavour to restrain and diminish the influence of the Crown, and prevent it from destroying those constitutional defences of the rights of the people, which are found in a state of representation directly and purely emanating from themselves."[76] Durham suggested a broad program of reforms in this speech, including redistricting and an extended franchise. His object, he argued, was to restore the "balance" of the constitution; the bill he proposed was not an innovation. "I ask for no privileges which have not already been enjoyed by our ancestors and to which I do not consider their posterity as entitled on every ground both of justice and expediency."[77] He used the same language in the Great Reform Bill debates, as we have seen, arguing that "we have not introduced anything new or unknown to our Constitution." The object of the bill, he said, was to "give security to the three estates."[78]

In 1821, 1832, 1834, and 1837 we find him putting forward the same doctrine: King, Lords, and Commons. In the year before the Canada mission, Durham is still affirming the position he had first taken as an outspoken member of the House of Commons. British North America was without the classes or orders implied by the term "estates," but in Durham's view that was no impediment to the establishment of mixed government. He seeks a "balance" of the powers of government in the colonies – the executive, upper house, and lower house – always representing his reforms as the expression of traditional principles. "Harmony" and "balance" are the words he uses to describe the system in which the branches are interacting, each checking the special interests and tendencies of the others, and all, as a consequence, promoting the general good: "Nor can I conceive that it would be found impossible or difficult to conduct a Colonial Government with precisely that limitation of the respective powers which has been so long and so easily maintained in Great Britain."[79]

Thus Durham knew as well as the Radicals that the British aristocracy had economic and political interests that conflicted with those of the "people," that ministers of the Crown and members of the upper house often – perhaps usually – tried to use their positions to further the narrow interests of party, family, and class. Indeed, like the Radicals, he thinks in terms of the "few" and the "many" – *ceux qui pillent* and *ceux qui sont pillés* – although he seldom uses these terms. He may speak of the three estates, or orders, of British society, but at bottom, as we shall see, he has a twofold division in mind.

But where the Radicals associate all political ills with the rule of the "few," and see as the remedy the exclusion of this "sinister" minority from the political aggregate, Durham believes that the interests of the few must not count less than the interests of the many – and, indeed, that to benefit the people, government requires the representatives of both few and many. He fears the rule of the few – in eighteenth-century language, "simple aristocracy" – no less than the Radicals, but he is most conscious of the possible dangers in the rule of those purporting to represent the many.

The Radicals treated the distinction between the few and the many as a function of social class. In their view, it was hereditary land, wealth, and privilege that corrupted the aristocracy and rendered their interests "separate and sinister." They argued that once "separate" interests were excluded, the pure and uncorrupted will of the "people" would shine forth – a coherent, universal interest on which legislation for the common good could be grounded.

But Durham treats the distinction as natural. All men may be greedy, but some, a few, are naturally very much greedier – greedy on another scale. And because the distinction is natural, it will appear in every social rank. For this reason he believes that there can be no hope of achieving a coherent popular interest merely by excluding the high-born and wealthy. The lowest rank of society will comprise any number of diverse competing interests, headed by ambitious and aggressive men hoping to climb the social and political ladder. Durham almost never refers to the "lower class" or the "middle class," in the style of twentieth-century writers. He speaks of the labouring classes and the middle classes, using the plural, and the usage, common among whigs and others, reflects the supposition that these ranks are composed of many not-easily reconcilable interests.[80]

In his view, the few and the many desire the same political objects –

possessions, security, freedom – but the many hope chiefly for security ("tranquillity" as he sometimes calls it) in which to enjoy possessions, while the few are endlessly ambitious and will give up tranquillity to attain their desires. There are natural thieves and natural victims; some men are predators and some are prey. "As long as personal ambition is inherent in human nature, and as long as the morality of every free and civilized community encourages its aspirations, it is one great business of a wise Government to provide for its legitimate development."[81]

Durham gives several pictures of the troublesomely ambitious "few." In his description of the assimilation of the populace of Louisiana, they are the "aspiring" men of French origin who found the rewards of governing Louisiana insignificant compared with the interests involved in politics in Washington. Whereas the rank and file of the French in Louisiana were satisfied with merely imitating the commercial habits of the English, the "aspiring" men were moved by ambition for political office.[82] The ambitious men, again, are the American adventurers ready to promote "undisguised projects of conquest" in Texas and the Canadas.[83] In the British colonies they are the disloyal leaders among the English-speaking populace who wished to rule a territory larger than the "small and unimportant communities" in which they found themselves.[84] And, most important, they are the French assembly leaders in Lower Canada, able to consider going to war because they believed they had been denied political office consonant with their talents.

The idea that some men are stronger, natural predators, and some weaker, natural prey, derives from ancient theories based on suppositions about human inequality.[85] Whig insights about the dangers of ambition are a distant reflection of the classic teaching in ancient political thought that some men are more fit to rule than others. But in whig writings the teaching about the "few" has been modified in order to make it fit with modern principles; it has been forced into the mould of equality of right. Nothing in what Durham says about the "few" is meant to justify inequality before the law or privileges for the few transcending the law. He is not describing a natural aristocracy, that is, men who are better than the mass of the people, but something more like a natural class of bullies. The Benthamites hoped that the absence of a conventional aristocracy in the colonies would smooth the way for majoritarian democracy. But if Durham had no trouble prescribing the mixed regime for colonies without a landed class or great differences between rich and poor, it was because he believed that one could always count on a natural crop of ambitious and able troublemakers.

His proposals for reform in Britain show him thinking along the same lines. He was one of those who argued for creation of peers as occasion demanded.[86] In an address to his home constituents in 1837, he urged a process of continuous appointment of men of "capacity and character," men "who are in touch with the enlightened and progressive aspirations of the nation."[87]

In short, the upper house was not to be composed solely of those with inherited wealth and titles. It was to include the ambitious from other classes as well. The presence of the three estates in Britain might explain the genesis of mixed government there, but it was not the function of the system to represent the estates as such, in Durham's opinion. As a branch of the mixed constitution, the upper house was to have a degree of independence, exactly as the executive branch was independent. He opposed the suggestion, common in British politics in the 1830s, for an elective Lords. In a letter, to Joseph Parkes in 1836, for example, he argued that the upper chamber "should be exempt from the influences which operate naturally on those who are chosen by particular bodies or constituencies."[88]

In keeping with these views, he proposed to abolish the one British institution in the colonies for which social rank seemed to be an absolute prerequisite – the institution of justices of the peace. In England, he noted, justices of the peace were subject to the moral responsibility imposed by their rank and the check exercised by other members of their class. But no such restraints operated in the colonies, and he concluded that the office was inappropriate there.[89] This was an instance where social rank was important; without the social basis, the institution was not feasible. The same conditions might have been thought to affect the position of candidates for the upper house. But it was Durham's opinion that in the case of the legislators, what counted were ambition and ability, natural qualities.

The "few," then, the "aspiring" men, the men of "capacity and character," will be found in the cabinet, the upper house, and the lower. They staff all the branches of the "balanced" constitution and head the factions in the upper house, and the diverse interests in the lower. They lead both the party of the few and the party of the many. When all is working well, under conditions of "balance," their own ambitions prompt them to check and thwart each other, so that no one individual or faction comes to dominate. The problem in Lower Canada was that the ambitious men representing the mass of the population had been able to exercise power virtually unchecked. Lower Canada was on the road to democracy, and the first evils were already evident.

Like many political thinkers who deplored the democratic trend of the period, Durham seems to have had two pictures of the conditions that would obtain under that regime – one in which individuals and factions battle lawlessly for scarce goods, and another in which all competition has ceased and all obey one ruler or party. Perhaps we are meant to think of these two together. In the worst state, citizens will quarrel more and more fiercely about matters of less and less consequence. At any rate, Durham described the problems of the lower province along two seemingly different lines.

He suggested, in the first place, that the strongest evidence of poor government in Lower Canada was the unseemly "scramble for local appropriations," a practice he refers to as "so vicious, and so productive of evil, that I believe until it is eradicated, representative government will be incapable of working well and smoothly in those Colonies." It served chiefly, he argued, to give "an undue influence to particular individuals or parties."[90] The assembly of Lower Canada, in his description, was preoccupied with the business of providing public money for small local requirements in each constituency. The preoccupation was the more unseemly because the assembly party had been unable to develop and implement the broad programs that would have obviated the need for local appropriations. Because there was no agricultural policy, for example, famine relief grants were handed out piecemeal. The assembly party had no schools policy, but provided support for this school or that, as the occasion demanded.[91] Even in the case of Upper Canada, as we have seen, Durham believed that assembly members were "ignorant of the real character of the general interests entrusted to their guardianship" and were "intent only on promoting sectional objects."[92]

The Radicals attributed the inability of the Lower Canada assembly to devise a coherent legislative program to the obstructive tactics of the "official party" in the legislative and executive councils. They could not suppose that Papineau's majority party, representing the mass of the people, was to blame because they believed that a coherent, universal interest could be found in the "whole uncorrupted portion of the people."[93] If the patriotes had been unable to legislate in the popular interest then, it could only be because the minority in the councils was exerting a malign influence. Durham, in constrast, did not think of a coherent interest as the basis of good government, but as the result, and he located the problem in the assembly, taking the assembly party to task.

It would not be true to say that he believed the assembly members were themselves to blame. He did not find fault with their intentions. He described each member as bent on securing the highest political returns for himself. But with such motives, as I have suggested, he had no quarrel. The difficulty, in his view, was that under the constitution of the colonies, the assembly members were positively rewarded for thinking in terms of piecemeal benefits and not large programs. Because the assembly members had little or no chance to rise to executive office, that is, because they could hope for no result more gratifying than re-election to the lower house, currying favour with the localities at the expense of the common good was the most profitable course for each man.

Consequently, a system was required in which each member could entertain hopes of a cabinet position: in short, the mixed constitution and "responsible government." The prospect of advancement would teach all to think in "larger" terms and secure the support for the executive that would enable it to proceed in vigorous style. Each member's need to consider local interests would not be less under "responsible government," but it would be to his advantage to support programs benefiting the locality only where they appeared to benefit the larger community as well. The same low, self-seeking motives that had resulted in the "vicious" system of "local appropriations" would then lead to exemplary results. The special alchemy of parliamentary debate in a system of checks and balances would turn those many competing interests in the assembly into measures for the common good.

But the disorder resulting from "local appropriations" and the dominance of partial and particular interests were not the worst consequences of Lower Canada's move to democracy. To the extent that assembly members were still trying to please their constituents, the full consequences of the system had not developed. It is when Durham refers to the French party leaders as "demagogues" and "agitators" that we begin to see what he most fears.[94] For in fact, the patriotes had little or no need to curry favour in the constituencies in order to secure re-election. Because they were the French-speaking candidates, connected with the electors "by all the associations of early youth ... ties of blood" and "community of interest," they appeared as the only possible party. The lack of "responsible government" and an independent executive militated against the development of a strong government. By implication it also worked to prevent the appearance of a strong opposition party. The appeal to nationality exacerbated this problem. It made opposition virtually impossible. Where "every contest is one of French and English in the outset, or becomes so ere it has run its course," no opposition party could arise in the French camp.[95] And it was this fact above all – that the "many" were tied to leaders acting in their name against whom they had no formal means of appeal – that had put Lower Canada on the road to tyranny.

In Durham's view, the leaders of both parties, French and English, had found it useful to invoke national prejudices. But the Radicals, with their views of the unspotted purity of the people's will and the people's duly elected representatives, could not entertain such a picture of the patriotes. Roebuck sees the patriote leaders as fit in every way to represent the "many" faithfully. They are *of* the "many." Durham holds that all political leaders, in any rank, any branch of government, must be recognized as of the "few" – potential tyrants. He appears to regard it as inevitable that a party unable to gratify the electorate's political and economic demands would seize on such a powerful tool as nationality. Certainly he believed that to suppose ties of blood and community enough to keep leaders true to the people was the height of foolishness.

Durham's full analysis of the abuses of nationality appears in the next chapter. Here it is enough to note that he surely supposed that the introduction of "responsible government" in the parliament of the united Canadas would divide the assembly, as the House of Commons was divided in England, into government party and opposition.[96] Under the simple representative system of the Radicals, the few would become tyrants. But under conditions of "balance," they would become conscientious and able governors and administrators. For if the "few" are natural thieves, then following the adage, other thieves may be set to catch them. A strong executive, to which assembly members can "aspire," will prompt some in the assembly to support the executive. The strength and independence of the executive makes the prize worthwhile. But since high positions on the government side are always in short supply, it can be supposed that some members will seek to supplant, not support, government leaders.

Like the government members, opposition members will have one eye on the constituencies and the other on the "large" chance. However, because their place is the popular house, in the British system they must mount all their criticism in the name of popular interests.[97] Under conditions of "balance," some aspiring men will always find that they must seek the popular platform and make popular interests their vehicle. Their affection for the people, or loyalty to their own background, need play no part. "King, Lords and Commons" ensures the representation of popular interests. And like a good machine, the system runs on cheap fuel – the ubiquitous motives of greed and ambition.

Thus, Durham believed that the ambitious few could be restrained only by enabling them to govern under a constitution that mixed more-representative and less-representative institutions. Nothing was more important than to enable the French-speaking "demagogues" of Lower Canada, the very men who had brought the government in the province to a standstill and provoked rebellion, to take their place in a strong, relatively independent executive council. He argued that a special precaution – the union of the Canadas – was needed to make sure that neither French nor English found it advantageous to appeal to nationality. But he clearly expected the British constitution to operate in the style of the home country after union. That system would mean that some ambitious men, French-speaking and English-speaking, who were left behind in the legislature would set out to depose their rivals; they would find the popular platform necessary and begin at last to "bring the influence of a vigorous public opinion to bear on every detail of public affairs."

The retention of the legislative councils was to make assurance doubly sure. Another institution whose members had a degree of independence because they were nominated and tenured, but who were at the same time without the power to obstruct indefinitely, would be an additional safeguard, another source of salutary opposition.[98]

It is clear that "balance" as espoused by the British thinkers has the same roots as the American doctrine of the separation of powers – the system of "checks and balances." That exact phrase is not used by Durham, but other whigs of the period did not hesitate to describe the British constitution in that language.[99] It is not surprising, then, to find that Tocqueville, describing the American institutions of the 1830s, sounds at times much like the British whigs: "Ce qui me répugne le plus en Amérique, ce n'est pas l'extrême liberté qui y règne, c'est le peu de garantie qu'on y trouve contre la tyrannie." In more than one passage he entertains the whig remedy: "Supposez ... un corps législatif composé de telle manière qu'il représente la majorité, sans être nécessairement l'esclave de ses passions; un pouvoir exécutif qui ait une force qui lui soit propre ... vous aurez encore un gouvernement démocratique, mais il n'y aura presque plus de chances pour la tyrannie."[100] In fact, he had doubts about the efficacy of British mixed government. Tocqueville's criticisms of British politics are much like Durham's: the executive in Britain has been so aggrandized that the popular element has become insufficient. But he is less sanguine about the probability of success in attempts to reform the system.[101]

Tocqueville looks to social institutions in addition to political – the growth of voluntary associations, for example, the study of law and of the classics – to preserve in an egalitarian society something of aristocratic tastes, perspectives, and talents. By this means, individual voices raised in opposition to government policies can be strengthened, preventing the decline into mediocrity, mob rule, and tyranny. In these views he shows himself less hopeful than Durham that the operation of a good constitution will in itself promote government in the interest of the mass of the people. It is true that both Durham and Tocqueville suggest that the inhibitions inculcated by religious instruction should be maintained in liberal society. It could be argued that Durham, too, shows some lack of faith in the efficacy of political institutions alone. In general, however, he sees less need for social supports than does Tocqueville. But their underlying thought is the same: the extremes of democracy lead to tyranny.

That this tendency would be exacerbated by the appeal to nationality is Durham's chief insight.

CHAPTER SEVEN

The Assimilation Proposal: Durham's Analysis

In the opening pages of the Report, Durham says that his English readers may have difficulty understanding and accepting his analysis of the crisis in Lower Canada.[1] He says that he himself had found the true explanation of the crisis hard to accept at first. "A quarrel based on the mere ground of national animosity, appears ... revolting to the notions of good sense and charity prevalent in the civilized world."[2] He represents his conclusions about Lower Canada as something that he could never have predicted from his knowledge of the politics of England and Europe and from the information about Canada that he had received in England: "I had still, in common with most of my countrymen, imagined that the original and constant source of the evil was to be found in the defects of the political institutions of the Provinces; that a reform of the constitution, or perhaps merely the introduction of a sounder practice into the administration of the government, would remove all causes of contest and complaint."[3] Only reluctantly, he suggests, and not until some time after his assumption of office in Canada did he conclude that "the contest, which had been represented as a contest of classes, was, in fact, a contest of races."[4] As he puts it in the most often quoted passage in the Report: "I expected to find a contest between a government and a people: I found two nations warring in the bosom of a single state: I found a struggle, not of principles, but of races."[5]

There is something puzzling about the notion conveyed by these famous lines. As I argued in chapter one, the suggestion that minorities must assimilate is implicit in liberal thought from the seventeenth century. It had certainly been discussed in concrete terms in debates on Canadian affairs long before Durham arrived on the scene. There was nothing new in 1838 about the idea that the quarrel of French and English was at the root of the problem in Lower Canada, and nothing new about the assimilation proposal. William Ormsby points out, for example, that Lord John Russell, Lord Melbourne, and others in the whig government were familiar with the suggestion that assimilation was the best course.[6] The very measure that Durham favoured, the union of the Canadas, had been put to the British Parliament first in 1822, and had debated at length in Britain and the colonies then and in the years after.

There is considerable evidence to show that Durham had made up his mind on this matter before he left England. Charles Buller tells us that his conversations with Durham on the voyage over showed Durham to be convinced then that "no quarter should be shown to the absurd pretensions of race, and that he must ... aim at making Canada thoroughly British."[7] Some historians have suggested that representations from the merchants of Montreal, laid before Durham in the period immediately before his departure, were a decisive influence.[8] The merchants were the most outspoken colonial group in favour of assimilation and the union of the Canadas, and certainly made every effort in the early months of 1838 to convince him to opt for union.[9]

In the introductory pages of the Report, then, Durham seems to have misrepresented his own position. The assimilation proposal was not new, and he did not come to it solely as the result of his Canadian experiences. We might say, in fact, that the problem with the assimilation proposal was precisely not that it was new or unfamiliar but that it was old and only too familiar. I suggest that this gives us a clue to Durham's intentions in ascribing to himself, in this section, views he never in fact held. He does it in order to appeal to the Radicals and to those in the colonies who might have been persuaded by them – chiefly, I would argue, the members of the French party in Lower Canada. The Report's opening section is addressed to the Radicals and the patriotes.

It was the Radicals who maintained that the source of the ills of the lower province could be traced to defects in the colonial constitution alone and that constitutional or administrative reform would suffice to remedy the problem. It was the Radicals who believed that the Canadian problem should be described simply as a "contest between a government and a people." They denied outright that "race" was a factor. In no sense could the quarrel in Canada be called a "contest of races," declared J.T. Leader during the debates on the Canadian question in March 1837 in the British House of Commons. Roebuck argued that "this is not a quarrel of races but a quarrel of principle."[10] For the Radicals it was a contest of principle, not "races"; for Durham, a contest of "races," not principles.

We might see Durham's device in these opening pages of the document as a clever variation on an old trick. Politicians introducing reforms often assert that their measures are in fact only variations on old themes and that their position conforms to old and valued principles. Who can doubt that the British whigs in the debates of 1830–2 revelled in the sheer political usefulness of the argument that by promoting parliamentary reform they were merely upholding the constitution of 1688? As we have seen, Durham, too, favoured this mode of argument in his British reform speeches. And as long as he was discussing constitutional measures, he used it in the Report, too: old programs are better, he suggests; the tried and true is preferable. On the subject of political reform he could perhaps not have abandoned this line. His record in Britain was too well known. For years he had prefaced his pleas for parliamentary reform with avowals never to depart from his whig principles and in particular never to yield to modish Radical arguments.[11]

But he may have concluded that the appeal to old principles was of limited use in North America. There was no golden age in the colonies' past.[12] It is certain, at any rate, that in the opening section of the Report, he presented his analysis of Lower Canada as if it were newer than new. He turns the old device inside out. He gives his arguments against the Radicals as the result of a dramatic conversion in his own thought. He suggests that he once believed that institutional remedies alone would suffice; he was later forced to recognize the significance of "race." He was once entirely in sympathy with the Radicals – and with the position of the patriotes, as the Radicals presented it – but after taking office, his practical experience prompted a superior view.

Later in the Report, Durham virtually confesses that he had never in fact succumbed to the Radical argument. We know from Buller that Durham had studied a number of important Canadian historical documents while he was still in England and on the voyage over. In a survey of Quebec's constitutional history, which he inserts at the end of his first analysis of the problems of the province, Durham reviews this material. The discussion is meant to serve as a critique of British rule but it is also inescapably an indication to careful readers that the assimilation proposal was not born in the instant, forced on him by his Canadian experiences, as he had suggested in the earlier section. Every passage that he quotes from the documents touches on the subject of nationality and gives the idea that this had always been the greatest issue in British North America.[13] He acknowledges in this section that his ideas are in part, or perhaps largely, a consequence of his reflection on the observations and recommendations of previous governors and officials in Lower Canada, officials in the Colonial Office, colonial subjects, and his whig associates in Britain; in this way he leads us to conclude that his pose as a convert to the Radical camp was rhetorical. It was a way to depict the Radical position as only superficially plausible and to put forward his own views as a carefully thought-out advance on the most progressive ideas of the time.

It is not always realized how much of the Report is a response to the Radicals. Point by point Durham addresses the Radical program. Roebuck argued for elective legislative councils and elective executive councils; Durham argued against.[14] Roebuck attributed all the ills of the colony to the English "official" party and singled out the legislative council for his most scathing comments. He favoured all reforms that would enhance the powers of the legislative assembly. Durham, in contrast, was alarmed by the ambitions of the legislative assembly and the attempt to elevate the assembly to supreme power. Roebuck believed that Papineau's party had attracted the support of both French and English in the colony.[15] Durham argued that by 1838 there were no longer English-speaking sympathizers among the patriotes.[16] He maintained that as the years passed, the line between the parties had been drawn more sharply on the basis of "race." Roebuck argued against the union of the Canadas and worked for measures that would increase the independence of the lower province. In circumstances where it seemed imprudent to argue for outright independence, he endorsed the union of the several colonies – believing that it would give Lower Canada more autonomy than union with Upper Canada alone.[17] Durham chose the union of the Canadas and rejected the idea of the larger union for the immediate future. He argued that the larger union would merely isolate Lower Canada, leaving the French and English parties to go on fighting, with ever more unhappy consequences for the mass of the population.[18] The disagreements, it can be seen, centre first on questions of constitutional reform and then on the matter of nationality in a reformed society. The whig analysis yielded one understanding of the problem of nationality; the Radical view, another.

To see the difference in these positions on nationality, we must note first that Roebuck as much as Durham represented what I have called the "mainstream" position. Both believed that assimilation was inevitable and just. Both held that individuals will abandon tradition when they are offered prospects for modernization, and that laws promoting nationality can only work to the disadvantage of minorities. But it was Roebuck's view that as assimilation progresses, nationality matters less. He maintained that the French Canadians had left their attachment to the old French laws and institutions far behind. In an article in *The Westminster Review* in 1835, he suggested, for example, that "in everything except language, and a few inconvenient laws, the population of Lower Canada is essentially English."[19] The French in Canada, he argued in another piece from 1836, have no desire "to maintain in predominance French customs and laws ... and ... prevent any innovation which savours of English habits, manners or feelings." They have, he went on, "no blind and prejudiced admiration of their own laws and customs ... They do not desire to retain such parts of them as are opposed to the improvement of the country."[20] Durham, in contrast, argued that even as assimilation went on, questions of nationality might come to usurp all other political matters. He maintained that the fact of modernization and assimilation had not precluded the growth of nationalist sentiments in Lower Canada. It is this contention and this point of difference with Roebuck that the rhetoric of the opening pages of the Report is meant to highlight.

Roebuck thought of Papineau's party as more advanced than any other colonial party, or any European party. It is hardly an exaggeration to say that he believed that the English should assimilate to Papineau's position.

He certainly thought that all right-thinking men – French, English, and even American – were flocking to Papineau's banner.[21] He insisted that there were no real political or economic differences between the French and the English at the popular level. "The truth is," he wrote, "that the division of the people is not into French and English, but into friends of popular government, and friends of government by a small body of place holders."[22] Papineau was entitled to govern, in Roebuck's opinion, because he was the leader who represented the aspirations of the majority, French speaking and English. It was on this basis, I have suggested, that the Radicals did all they could in the spring of 1838 to work for the defeat of the British in Lower Canada, and to win British sympathy for that defeat.

When Roebuck deigned to take note of the fact that the language of "race" dominated most political debates in the province, he argued that it was the English party alone that was fomenting these sentiments. He held that the English "official" party were systematically promoting the idea of French nationality in order to subordinate the French, and to prevent the mass of the people, French and English, from seeing their common enemy.[23] Not for Roebuck was the idea that the French as well as the English had found the appeal to nationality useful.

Roebuck's conclusion follows from his constitutional doctrine. He was sure that a majority party would generate only wholesome sentiments. He could not believe that majority party leaders would stoop to low tricks, even when, like the leaders of the French party in Lower Canada, they had been treated unjustly. But Durham, who has no special trust for majority leaders, does not think that securing a majority endows an elite with virtue or purity. Majority leaders especially must be subject to the checks and balances of the parliamentary system. He had no trouble entertaining the idea that the French as well as the English had found the appeal to nationality a useful tool in the political struggle. "Every contest is one of French and English in the outset," he wrote, "or becomes so ere it runs its course"; a "deadly animosity ... separates the inhabitants of Lower Canada into the hostile divisions of French and English."[24] Roebuck concludes that because all the provinces suffer from the same ills, one remedy will suffice for all; while Durham maintains that for Lower Canada special measures are required. Means must be found to wean the English elite in the province from appealing to their national sense of superiority and the French from capitalizing on their national sense of resentment.[25]

Durham uses the terms "race" and nationality to refer to both the old way of life as it was in Quebec at the time of the conquest and to the new sentiment he saw rising in the province in the 1830s. Nevertheless, we are entitled to conclude that he had in mind a distinction between the new sentiment and the old. As I noted before, he sometimes spoke as if the mass of the French Canadians still lived in a traditional society: "The conquest has changed them but little ... they remain an old and stationary society"; but in the course of his analysis he typically points to factors that suggest that French society had undergone a sharp change. He noted that the inhabitants of the seigneuries were moving to the cities.[26] He argued that education was once despised by the mass of the people and was now generally sought after.[27] He suggested that many saw the rebellions not so much as a way of throwing off English rule as a way of ridding themselves of "feudal burthens."[28] The very fact that the French could take up arms against authority showed how much they had changed from the authority-ridden people of old. French-Canadian society had changed and so had the character of French-Canadian allegiance to things French. The original national feeling and loyalty to the French tradition had waned – assimilation had indeed advanced in the manner predicted by liberal theory – and in their stead had come a new form of nationality compatible with the fact of assimilation.

The new nationality, he believed, was the deliberate creation of leading political figures in the French party who saw the evocation of national sentiment as the best means (perhaps the only means) to attach the mass of the people to the French party in the assembly, and so secure their own election and their own utterly personal goals. He thought of nationality in Lower Canada in the 1830s as the product of men attempting to achieve the goals typical of liberal society, that is, of men already assimilated to the prevailing North American "manners." If the nationality they fostered had something of the aura of the old nationality, because it used the old names and recalled the old emotions, it was undoubtedly stronger for that; but it was in its origins and character markedly different from the old: new wine in old bottles. The old form of nationality in French Canada had restrained men's passions and subjected individuals to the common good; the new is subject to the individual, one of the means by which he achieves his personal aims. The old we have described as the regime of "virtue"; the new is compatible with the regime of "freedom and civilization."[29]

An apparently continuing loyalty to nationality in a modernizing society is not, therefore, in Durham's view, a plea for reversion to traditional ways, or a counterweight to assimilation, but an expression of the very process of assimilation. What purported to be a movement of opposition to assimilation in Lower Canada in the 1830s was in reality quite the opposite. Where Roebuck holds, in straightforward fashion, that national loyalties decrease with assimilation, Durham argues that the political use of national feelings may increase with assimilation.

In the years immediately after the conquest, Durham argues, the two nations were utterly unlike in "character and temperament ... language, laws, and modes of life."[30] The French-Canadian way of life dated from before the revolution in France; it was a distant echo of the "great nation, that for two centuries gave the tone of thought to the European Continent," shaped by the "repressive despotism" of French colonial rule.[31] The English, in contrast, represented the modern, commerical civilization destined to inherit the New World. He may describe the English officials as contemptuous and intolerant and the labouring classes as ignorant and demoralized; nevertheless, he believed that as a people they possessed the practical sagacity and energy in politics needed by those concerned in the government of themselves.

It was hardly to be expected that friendship would bloom immediately. "A jealousy between two races, so long habituated to regard each other with hereditary enmity, and so differing in habits, in language and in laws, would have been inevitable under any form of government."[32] Jealousy had characterized relations between French and English in Louisiana, as well, in the early years. And again, in Louisiana just as in British North America, jealousy had prompted the mass of the people to seek wealth and the educated classes to seek positions of power and prestige. But in the United States, nothing prevented the French from competing in business, and nothing prevented the leading men in the French community from taking their places in the government that was, as Durham notes, greater in size and prestige than any British colony.[33] "Every provision was made in Louisiana for securing to both races a perfectly equal participation in all the benefits of the Government.[34] The competition that began with jealousy proved the means to resolve the cause of jealousy.

In Canada matters had developed otherwise. The able and educated among the French suffered from the first under what Durham calls the English system of "exclusion." "Unjust favouritism" deprived the French of those positions in government and in the legal profession to which their experience and education entitled them.[35] Although Durham notes that at first some among the French population appeared to share the prosperity of the English society, it was chiefly as employees that they felt these benefits. The mass of the people, confined to feudal seigneuries gradually becoming overpopulated under the old laws of inheritance, became ever more aware that the English were better off.[36]

Two factors in particular exacerbated this development: increasing English immigration and the grant of representative institutions.[37] Each contributed toward making the French more aware of their deprivations and of the fact that they could not surmount them. The success of English in agriculture became more evident as the populations came, slowly, to live in the same area of the province.[38] With the establishment of representative government, the French majority was given what was apparently substantial legislative power. But it was this grant of legislative power that made them aware of their exclusion from executive office. Thus, while the populace was led to desire a prosperity constantly denied them, their leaders were brought to see the advantages of political powers forever, as it seemed, beyond their grasp. Just as in Louisiana, the French began to seek the same goals as their

English neighbours and to abandon whole-hearted allegiance to the old customs and "manners"; but because the new goals were unattainable, jealousy between the peoples assumed new proportions even as the process of assimilation went on.

"I desire to give to the Canadians our English character," Durham writes, "for the sake of the educated classes, whom the distinction of language and manners keeps apart from the great Empire to which they belong." "I desire the amalgamation still more," he goes on, "for the sake of the humbler classes" for "their present state of rude and equal plenty is fast deteriorating."[39]

Casting his distrustful eye on the ambitions of the political leaders, French and English, Durham distinguishes the objectives of the French party leaders from those of the mass of the French people, and the objectives of the English party from those of the English settler population.

What was most confusing about the dispute in the 1830s for an outside observer, he tells us more than once, was the fact that the public position of the French assembly party betrayed no sympathy for the French nationality or the French cause as such. Because the assembly party represented the majority, he writes, they "have invoked the principles of popular control and democracy, and appealed with no little effect to the sympathy of liberal politicians in every quarter of the world."[40] But this was their public face. When we look at their tactics in the legislative assembly, he goes on, we seldom find them favouring liberal goals; on the contrary, he says, they "used their democratic arms for conservative purposes, rather than those of liberal and enlightened movement." In the legislature the significance of nationality loomed large, and the real objectives of the leaders appeared to be some "vague expectation of absolute independence," some ill-defined hope of establishing "La Nation Canadienne."[41]

Even this is not the full story, in his opinion, for (as I have argued) he is far from thinking that the assembly party leaders had as their real objective "La Nation Canadienne." He believed that they cared very little or not at all for the preservation of their nationality, and he illustrates this in several ways. He cites, for example, what he understood to be the willingness of the French leaders to countenance union with the United States. An invading American army, he maintained, would have been welcomed in Lower Canada, despite the fact that the leaders of the party knew very well that their chances of preserving their way of life would be diminished by incorporation in the liberal society of the United States.[42]

Durham's analysis of the tactics of the French and the objectives of the assembly leaders reveals three levels. On the first, the assembly leaders appear liberal and progressive, perhaps because they could see as well as Durham that in the 1830s a "quarrel based on the mere ground of national animosity" appeared "revolting to the notions of good sense and charity prevalent in the civilized world."[43] On the second level, party leaders invoked national- ity, ostensibly in order to preserve their way of life. But their real objectives – and the third level of Durham's analysis – are revealed when we look more carefully at this appeal to nationality.

The three levels of the analysis and the full dimensions of the new contest of "races" are given their clearest exposition in his depiction of two impor- tant political issues of the 1830s: the project for the reform of the laws of land tenure, and the movement to establish a general system of education. No reforms were more needed than these, he suggests, but in each case the hostility of the "races" had rendered political action impossible.

The easy alienation of land, according to Durham, "is, in a new country, absolutely essential to its settlement and improvement."[44] Reform in this area was immediately needed if the crowded conditions in the traditional seigneu- ries, the debilitation of the land, and the increasing poverty of the populace at large were to be rectified. It appeared to some observers that the English favoured, and the French opposed, the commutation of feudal tenures and the establishment of offices for the registration of real estate in the English manner. Certainly the French had repeatedly thwarted these measures in the popular assembly. Yet Durham suggests that the real opposition and support on this issue were distributed otherwise. He writes: "It was among the ablest and most influential leaders of the English that I found some of the opponents of both the proposed reforms." He does not say, but he doubtless intends us to understand, that the Englishmen opposed to these reforms were among those who owned seigneuries. As he notes elsewhere, fully one-half of the valuable seigneuries were owned by Englishmen who were very often able to make profits from land that had not afforded wealth to French owners, and who often exercised their rights of ownership and made their profits "in a manner which would appear perfectly fair in [Britain], but which the Cana- dian settler reasonably regarded as oppressive."[45] At the same time, the Eng- lish community at large, as opposed to the wealthy English minority, was in favour of reform of land tenure.

The real position of the French on this issue was even more unexpected. In keeping with their public posture as leaders of a popular reform party, prominent French party men declared themselves "anxious to disclaim any hostility to these reforms." But they continued to reject efforts made by Durham to effect these reforms during his term as governor, just as they had opposed the reforms in the assembly in former years. This opposition was in keeping with the "conservative" purposes of the assembly party. As Durham argues, seigneurial tenure was one of the important traditions defining the French nationality. The fact that land was not easy to alienate at once promoted com- munities in which familial and national traditions were easily transmitted from one generation to the next, and discouraged the commercial development typi- cal of the English way of life.[46] The adoption of English laws of tenure might well have revolutionary consequences. Nevertheless, in Durham's opinion, assembly opposition to these reforms in reality had little to do with La Nation Canadienne. He believed that the stand of the French leaders was not in any way a response to needs or wishes expressed by the French people, but had to do with the desire of the assembly leaders to oppose any and all measures generally thought to be part of the English party's program. He was convinced that among the French population at large there was substantial support for this reform. The "mass of the French population" had "exhibited, in every possible shape, their hostility to the state of things which their leaders had so obstinately maintained."[47] He admits that many of the habitants themselves were opposed to reform, but he suggests that the issue had been obscured deliberately for these people, so that those who lived on the land and should therefore have been most interested in the success of the reforms, had been rendered unable to see where their interest lay. He argues that the artisans and labourers among the French favoured land reform outright, and concluded that in the French population as a whole, there was to be found a majority who could perceive the benefits to be gained from these measures.[48]

The French leaders in the assembly, then, had taken up a position opposing reforms that would have benefited many people, reforms that were desired by their own followers, because they had come to think of land reform as an English measure, part of the English party's program. The irony was that their stand worked to the advantage of some of the most influential of the English-speaking colonists, the ones that had discovered the uses of feudal tenure in a modern economy. Durham points to the real motives behind the assembly party's stand:

When I observe the inconsistencies of conduct among the opponents and supporters of these reforms ... I cannot but think that many, both of the supporters and of the opponents, cared less for the measures themselves, than for the handle which the agitation of them gave to their national hostility; that the Assembly resisted these changes chiefly because the English desired them; and that the eagerness with which many of the English urged them was stimulated by finding them opposed by the French.[49]

The position taken by the French and English parties had nothing to do with their avowed programs, nothing to do with their perception of the wishes of their people, or the common good, and every thing to do with their own narrow struggle for political position.

The proposal for a system of general education is a second example illustrating Durham's idea of the new character of the feud between French and English. About the prospect of establishing a system of schools, he writes: "I was rejoiced to find that there existed among the French population a very general and deep sense of their own deficiencies in this respect, and a great desire to provide means for giving their children those advantages which had been denied to themselves. Among the English the same desire was equally felt."[50] Here, as in the instance of land tenure, there was the consensus needed for legislation. It was a mark of the degree to which assimilation had progressed that education (not desired by the French in the early years after the conquest, as Durham believed) was now appreciated as a necessity. He professes to have seen among the laity of the province support for a secular system; whatever the character of the schools, secular or religious, however, everyone was anxious to see the children of the province taught to read and write.[51]

In his Commission of Inquiry into Education, written for Durham, Arthur Buller describes at length the interesting story of the legislative assembly's repeated attempts to establish a system of education, and Durham refers to these events several times. Despite the general desire for schools, and despite the professed good will of members of the assembly for this end, the popular house was never able to maintain a school system. Educational provisions under the supervision of the legislature, Buller notes, "were framed with a view to promote party rather than education."[52] Under the provisions of the Constitution Act of 1791, each assembly member found it more to his advantage to secure funds for his constituency than to work with others and the executive in a co-ordinated effort. According to Arthur Buller, schools opened and closed, and were provided or not provided with books, according to the fortunes of the party in the area, the party allegiance of the teacher, and the energies of the assembly member. The schools were part of the loot in what Durham called the unseemly "scramble for local appropriations."[53] But he appears to have thought that there was another aspect to this puzzling situation.

Durham suggests that it suited the assembly leaders to keep the mass of the French people ignorant. The under-educated habitants and the highly educated graduates of the seminaries lived, as he notes, in the same villages, in the same station of life, very often in the same family setting. "The circumstances of a new and unsettled country, the operation of the French laws of inheritance, and the absence of any means of accumulation, by commerce or manufactures, have produced a remarkable equality of properties and conditions."[54] It was, as I have said, exactly this situation that he saw as most dangerous. The young men of superior education and ambition preserved and cultivated their extraordinary influence with the people as their only means of attaining political power. From these educationally privileged ranks came the "Canadian demagogues," the "petty agitators" of the province.[55] Such a man, says Durham, "combines ... the influence of superior knowledge and social equality, and wields a power over the mass, which I do not believe that the educated class of any other portion of the world possess ... The most uninstructed population anywhere trusted with political power, is thus placed in the hands of a small body of instructed persons."[56]

The habitants, the artisans and working men, Durham says, had come to obey leaders "who ruled them by the influence of a blind confidence and narrow national prejudice."[57] He did not blame the French solely for the lack of schools. On the contrary, he thought that the responsibility for establishing a system of general education lay properly with the British administrators of Lower Canada.[58] It was not only the lack of schools, moreover, which kept the population ignorant. Municipal and local political institutions that would have provided a political education had also been denied the people, and this was clearly the fault of the colonial administration. What was surprising, however, was that the effective policies of the administration, and the policies of the French party leaders ostensibly opposed to the administration, coincided exactly.

The example of the province's failure to effect land-tenure reforms illustrated the fact that leaders of the French party did not represent the political and economic demands of the French population. The example of the failure to establish schools indicated that without speaking for the people on political issues, the French party was nevertheless able to hold its place. The patriote leaders were able to ignore the interests and the needs of their dependents and rely instead on the unthinking allegiance that followed on nationalist appeals. The assembly members made ill-coordinated attempts to work for the welfare of their constituents, but devoted their real energies to promoting the dependence of the electorate; at the same time, they attempted to magnify the powers of the popular house in modes, as Durham says, "totally incompatible with the principles of constitutional liberty."[59] He suggests, indeed, that the party leaders were inculcating the kind of docility and dependence that had characterized the French people during the years of French rule. They were developing a form of rule, he charges, as oppressive as that of old France – worse, in fact, because administered by popular leaders in the name of the people.

Thus, while the assembly leaders publicly professed their interest in a liberal program, they were driven in practice to oppose all measures identified with the English party, however liberal. On the surface the French party appeared to be liberal and popular in the best sense, a party speaking for the majority. On the second level, as I have called it, the party had a conservative face, opposing reform and supporting French-Canadian traditions. Both perceptions were wrong, in Durham's opinion. The party was not dedicated to popular interests, nor to the preservation of the old French-Canadian way of life. The French party elite were appealing to national feelings in order to justify their constant opposition to everything associated with the English, and to cement their relationship with the French-speaking voters. They were moved by personal ambition, not the desire to return to tradition; they were invoking nationality in the new form. On this deepest level the motives of the assembly party leaders were liberal, true enough; had Lower Canada been governed by good political institutions, the French leaders' ambition and desire for public office would have led them to champion the reforms desired by their followers. But given the conditions prevailing in the province, given that prospects for attaining public office were distant, the assembly party's quarrel with the English led them to betray the electorate. Their ambition pitted them against the mass of the people.

To match his analysis of the French party, Durham describes the English party's domination of the English settlers. There was a curious similarity between relations within the English camp and relations within the French. A "small knot" of English-speaking colonial officials in Lower Canada controlled the executive and administrative posts, while the English settler populace was in effect excluded from government altogether. Durham argues that the interests of the English settlers were closer to those of the French Canadians than to those of the office-holding English elite. But he suggests that although the English colonists were well aware of the deteriorating conditions in the province, and of their powerlessness to affect the situation, they were unable to see the advantages of alliance with their counterparts among the French.[60] The English saw the French party as monolithic, presenting a solidly nationalist front, resolutely opposed to political reform. Just as the mass of the French populace was tied to the French party leaders, so the mass of the English-speaking colonists was tied to the English elite, in what Durham calls a "singular alliance." The English were as badly represented by their leaders as the French by theirs: "Thus a bold and intelligent democracy was impelled, by its impatience for liberal measures ... to make common cause with a government which was at issue with the majority on the question of popular rights."[61]

Just as the real objectives of the French party were revealed by its willingness to condone incorporation into the American union, so the real objectives of the English party were revealed by its stand on this issue. The English professed a strong allegiance to British political traditions, the Crown, and empire; but, in fact, their hostility to the French brought many to think, Durham argues, that union with the Americans would not only enable them to share in "the amazing prosperity of the United States" but would also destroy their enemies, the French, as a nationality. He cites a current sentiment: "'Lower Canada must be *English*, at the expense, if necessary, of not being *British*.'"[62]

Thus, while the real political interests of English and French had begun to converge, the people of the province were arraigned in hostile parties, which claimed their loyalty by recreating the sense of national identification, by appealing to prejudice, and by confusing their sense of their own real interests. Because these parties ignored the real interests of the people and the economic issues of overriding importance in the province, they could not act, either in concert or independently, for the common good. Their partial purposes, in the absurd climax of the development of national hostility in Lower Canada, were no longer even those of the French nationality as such, or of the English nationality – but among the French, the senseless plans of "separate petty agitators," and among the English, projects for the betrayal of the laws and country to which they professed loyalty.[63]

Durham sees two minority factions – both irresponsible in the deepest sense – competing for power in the lower province: the English party entrenched in the executive branch and the French demagogues whose base was the assembly. The English faction will never submit to majority French rule; the French faction, denied legitimate opportunities for power, will not cease to promote rebellion. But in Durham's eyes, the increasing acrimony, the very competition then threatening to destroy peace, pointed to the solution. It was a sign of the growth of the "spirit of accumulation," the acceptance of the competitive, "money-making" way of life, the triumph of the modern influence. The patriote leaders had already assumed the habits, manners, and mode of life appropriate for leaders of a popular party in a liberal society. If they were not familiar with the business of government as such because they had been excluded from executive positions, they were only too skilled in the uses of the elective assembly in representative government. They had become as enterprising, calculating, and self-reliant as the English. That the French elite did not represent the French people was perhaps the most disruptive factor in the crisis; but under a just, liberal government, the very characteristics which at that time worked against order and good government would be harnessed for the common good. Identifying the mischievous character of the able and ambitious among the French was not grounds for excluding them from power. Rather the most important single factor in the remedy was to find a means to enable these men to exercise power in the popular house and in the executive, in a context where they could not and need not promote nationality in order to maintain power. ("As long as personal ambition is inherent in human nature ... it is one great business of a wise Government to provide for its legitimate development."[64]) The interests of the English party had also to be provided for, and in the new order they, too, must be placed so that they could not assert their claims on the basis of "race." "Responsible government" (as a principle of the balanced constitution) and the union of the Canadas were the remedies. In the united province, all would compete for executive positions on the basis of individual merit and persuasiveness, and "race" would be discounted. The English would no longer dominate one branch of government and the French the other. Some among the English and some among the French would become ministers of the Crown, while others of both nationalities would always find it necessary to sit in the popular house; and once there they would find it to their advantage to put forward popular claims.

When the French and English of the lower province were merged in the larger unit formed by the union, then the warring national parties would be destroyed, leaving only (as in Louisiana) "the ordinary animosities of party in a free country."[65] The appeal to the intolerant principle of "race" would be laid aside, just as the appeal to the intolerant principle of uncompromising religious authority had been laid aside long before in both Britain and the colonies. The able men of each nationality would then surely form new political alliances with men of the other "race" – French and English working together – in order to pursue their course in the larger arena. And given new parties and a reformed constitution, the real accord between the French and English populations would be revealed, enabling legislation for the common good.

Roebuck hoped to see the patriotes govern. "Power to the people," was his slogan; power to the majority. He meant to see Papineau govern and the official party turned out, apparently for the duration. But in Durham's view, no class or "race" can be excluded from the parliamentary process. In England, where the Radicals called for the exclusion of the aristocratic, "sinister," whig and tory minority, his response was always the same: "It has ... been my ruling principle throughout my political life to endeavour to bring all classes ... within the pale of the true ... constitution."[66]

Durham must have regarded Roebuck's remedy as simply unworkable. The truculent English officials of Lower Canada were not going to relinquish their offices without at least the prospect of gaining positions again under the new rules. The Radicals painted a picture of the "official" party as vicious and self-seeking, but appeared to think that they could be easily pushed aside by the pure in heart.

More important, from Durham's perspective, is that Roebuck had failed as well to see how the French elite had come to dominate their compatriots and to capitalize on their position by appealing to national loyalties. Roebuck concentrated on the patriotes'- status as leaders of the majority. In European eyes the electoral practices and suffrage in the colony were eminently fair.[67] Roebuck held fast to the idea that the party fairly elected by the mass of the people was entitled to power. He did not see that the assembly leaders had had to rely, not on their position as majority leaders, but on their position as members of the French community to maintain their power. His fine feeling for the trespasses of the English-speaking "official" party had blinded him to the emergence of a similar elite within the ranks of the patriotes, one potentially as oppressive. It was Durham's view that the French were now seeking to rule as French, just as the English had so often tried to rule as English. And he drew the mainstream conclusion, that the one was as intolerable as the other.

The debates about land tenure and schooling were undoubtedly critical in the 1830s. At the same time, Durham's treatment of these issues points to the idea that we should think more generally of laws and policies relating to land usage and education as defining a nationality. His analysis suggests that where individuals of any rank can own, buy, and sell land, and where all children are eligible for the education that will equip them to participate in the politics and economic life of the nation, we have a society of modern men, men assimilated to the prevailing way of life. He is clearly not thinking of language and political "style" as defining nationality, nor, as we so often do today, of private preferences and associations.[68]

From the discussion in chapters three and four, we can add that Durham singled out the laws of land usage and education as critical because they were church-related, that is, because they were part of an order justified by an appeal beyond political debate. The comparison with Tocqueville is useful again. I suggested earlier that Tocqueville is less sure than Durham that political debate alone will lift men from a narrow preoccupation with self to larger programs and national objectives. He worries that the extremes of "individualism" (his term) will leave men of the future unable to unite to combat injustice and preserve freedom. Accordingly, he looks for social factors to strengthen individual voices raised in opposition to tyranny. He favours diversity, regionalism, local government, federalism. He looks to family ties, voluntary associations, professional societies. He is seeking to establish in a society founded on the principle of equality, a counterpart to the bonds and social links of aristocracy, without re-establishing aristocracy and without appealing to any principle superior to popular consent. As one commentator remarks, Tocqueville tries to "solve the problem of democracy on the level of democracy."[69] It is the more illuminating, then, that nowhere throughout the two volumes of De la Démocratie does he put forward nationality or allegiance to particular cultural traditions as a remedy for the "tyranny of the majority." He is not sure that liberalism can furnish an adequate ground for political obligation and a commitment to "large" programs, but he does not point to nationalist sentiments as a corrective. In particular, he did not see the nationality of French Canada as something that the British should encourage or the French hope for.

Tocqueville's discussion of "great parties," and his comparison of the "great parties" of the revolutionary period with the "small parties" of nineteenth-century America, points to his thought on this matter.[70] He argues that "great parties" can have no place in modern liberal politics because they appeal beyond the sovereignty of the people, or the people's government.[71] It was typical of the "great parties," he says, to refer to a transcendent or universal principle, and such parties, he argues, are changed only by revolution or civil war. They rend and convulse society; they may bring in liberal and democratic government, or expel it. They may be nobler, bolder, less obviously devoted to petty, selfish interests, but they are incompatible with the principles of equality and liberalism. What liberal society requires are "small parties" – in Durham's term, "ordinary parties" – which are subject to the compromises of parliamentary debate, standing fast only on equality and tolerance. A nationality that could resist assimilation would surely have the character of a "great party" – and would be no more tolerable. Groups with the character of voluntary associations may be tolerated; loyalties of the deepest nature can no more be allowed an authoritative voice in politics than can priests and church hierarchies, and for the same reason.

As a politician writing a government report, Durham discusses concrete problems and proposes concrete remedies. He has few reasons to cast his conclusions in general form. But it is not difficult to read the underlying doctrine. Like so many modern thinkers, he has begun with the supposition that tradition must give way to modernity, the regime of "virtue" to the regime of "freedom and civilization." He does not altogether deny the worth of traditional society; many would find his picture of traditional French Canada attractive. He describes the French Canadians as "virtuous," "amiable," and "contented."[72] They were, he says, "mild and kindly ... distinguished for a courtesy and real politeness, which pervades every class of society." He argues that the "temptations which, in other states of society, lead to offenses against property, and the passions which prompt to violence, were little known among them." Their virtue, it would seem, was a function of their simple life, and of the "ancient prejudices, ancient customs and ancient laws" that encompassed them. It was a life that offered few temptations. Each habitant, he notes, "obtained his land on a tenure singularly calculated to promote his immediate comfort, and to check his desire to better his condition." There was no great gap between rich and poor. Most households were relatively self-sufficient: "the rude manufactures of the country were ... carried on in the cottage."[73] Hard work, simple social pleasures, self-sufficiency, equality – we could believe that Jean-Jacques Rousseau had invented this society. There was much to gratify in that way of life, and perhaps more important, little to promote dissatisfaction. "They are a people with no history, and no literature," writes Durham; they have no theatre, he notes, no national stage.[74] We can imagine Rousseau applauding; could there be a surer recipe for happiness and goodness? Durham is at least in part sensible of the benefits of that French-Canadian society.

But the laws that check ambition and promote "virtue" are exactly those that cannot be tolerated in liberalism. In keeping with liberal thought, Durham holds that "ancient prejudices ... ancient laws," church and hierarchy, are to have no prescriptive force in politics. For it is freedom, not "virtue," that he chooses. In his opinion, the life of freedom and "independence" is more "elevated" than the life of socially inculcated virtue. The restless, "demoralized" life of the English settlers was preferable to the happy goodness of the French Canadians.

At the same time, Durham appears sure that his readers, French and English, will also prefer the life of freedom. It will not be difficult to ban the "ancient prejudices." His readers will chose freedom, perhaps, because it is more "elevated," but also – certainly – because it promises unequalled prosperity. It is natural for the "many" to hope for wealth and the "few" for power, and these are the rewards promised by modernity. As we have seen, he argues that it was the promise of prosperity and power that lay behind the English-speaking colonists' "attachment" to the empire and parliamentary institutions; he warned the home-country government that the colonists' loyalty would wane as economic conditions in the colonies worsened. In the same way, he believed that the promise of prosperity and power in a reformed society would win the French Canadians from their "attachment" to the seigneuries and church schools. Where a society opens opportunities to all regardless of origin, then most men will see the advantage of giving up the laws and institutions that would hamper their full participation in the nation's politics and economy. Louisiana is the model; the "influence of perfectly equal and popular institutions" in that state, he argues, had effaced "distinctions of race without disorder or oppression."[75] Liberal policies and liberal justice erode traditional ways of life.

In those instances where a government, prompted perhaps by a vaguely generous impulse, or (more likely) by the desire to reinforce the privileges of the ruling "race," upholds minority traditions in law, members of the minority who find their opportunities curtailed may appeal to tradition or to collective rights, in "a spirit of jealous and resentful nationality" in order to press the claim to equal opportunity and full participation.[76] As they assert their right to liberal benefits, that is, as they adopt the modern way of life, leaders of minority peoples may find new uses for traditional sentiments. Traditional, ethnic, or nationalist claims are advanced as claims transcending parliamentary debate, as "intolerant" absolute claims, and assimilation and the "contest of races" escalate together. Durham admits that people may feel a regret at the loss of their nationality even as they discard it. It is their regret that may make them susceptible to leaders using the appeal to national traditions for their own ends. But no regret, no feeling for tradition, justifies laws or policies intended to promote deep-seated cultural differences. At best such schemes will deny individuals liberal opportunities. More likely they will prove a formula for violence or tyranny.

We cannot turn to Durham for an explanation or justification of the regime of "virtue." His work shows only the shadow of that society. What we find in his argument is reason to believe that the appeal to "virtue" erodes liberal freedoms, but reason to hope, nevertheless, that we can cherish the best aspects of our modern way of life, our rights, freedom, tolerance, and equality.

CHAPTER EIGHT

The Assimilation
Proposal:
Challenges

In recent years the mainstream position has been challenged from several quarters. Mainstream thinkers argued that a modern society must exhibit a degree of homogeneity, and that differences of language, habit, and custom will become matters of private life and private preference within nations predominantly liberal in character. Social scientists more often suggest now that ethnic and nationalist differences are too vital and too deeply entrenched to be contained in private associations, and that continuing cultural diversity is the most salient and perhaps the most welcome feature of the modern world. David Cameron argues for example, that the thinkers who believed that "the strength of nationalist sentiment would recede" were quite simply wrong.[1] In fact, he says, "nothing of the kind happened." McRoberts and Posgate argue that the observers who had assumed that modernization would erode Québécois feelings were surprised by the flourishing nationalism in the province in the 1960s and entirely unable to explain it.[2] In the opinion of these writers and others like them, mainstream liberal views on nationality must be revised or discarded.

Expressing this newer perspective, Kenneth McRae argues that the "mainstream" of Western political thought "has shown little understanding or respect for the cultural diversity of mankind, and has made scant allowance for it as a possible concern of government." "Hobbes made politics a science," he writes, "but a science that suppresses or subordinates every major source of human variation." We must "acknowledge cultural pluralism" and build on it, he goes on, "before the time for rational discussion runs out."[3] "Liberals and their historic doctrine neglect collective entities," according to Vernon Van Dyke: "Since the time of Hobbes and Locke, liberal political theorists have made it their primary purpose to explore relationships between the individual and the state." He concludes: "The requirements of logic and the long-term requirements of universal justice commend the idea of accepting communities as right-and-duty-bearing units."[4]

It is easy to forget how great and how striking this change in political thought has been.[5] It was only recently that politicians, in keeping with the principles of the mainstream, would typically represent the cause of minorities by demanding for their followers the rights said to be due to each and all in a modern society. Today they more often ask for collective rights and special status for their constituents, that is, rights as members of a caste, clan, tribe, ethnic, or nationalist group.[6]

To argue now that law and government should remain totally indifferent to community and collectivity, tribe and ethnic group, is taken as a mark of intolerance; it is not considered prudent, given the character of ethnic demands in modern nations, and more particularly, it is not considered just. But according to earlier liberal theory, it was exactly indifference to community and collectivity that was tolerant, prudent, and just. Discrimination on the basis of race, origin, colour, or creed – to use the famous liberal formulation – was regarded as the very definition of intolerance and injustice. This is not to say that discrimination was not practised in liberal societies in former days; far from it. But lack of discrimination was always recognized as the standard, and it is the standard that is now being challenged. To identify the individual in law with the community of his birth was formerly thought reprehensible and may now seem commendable.

In short, what was at issue in the old quarrel between Durham and his commentators in now the subject of debate in a larger arena. We could say that reinforcements have arrived for the historians' camp. It is true that Durham's commentators say nothing about what I have called the mainstream position, whereas McRae, Cameron, and Van Dyke write mainly to refute it; they see themselves as attacking a well-buttressed theoretical position. While the historians, as we have seen, tend to recommend changes in attitude to remedy nationalist quarrels, the mainstream revisionists argue that nothing less will do than far-reaching institutional changes. They propose group rights and may suggest that collectivities be represented in the legislature. But clearly the historians and the revisionists share common ground. They have a similar respect for nationalist and ethnic loyalties. If we take up the issues between the mainstream, represented by Durham, and the revisionists, we will not be leaving the commentators entirely behind. We should find that the best of the commentators' arguments are presented by the revisionists on more theoretical ground.

Moving into the larger arena, we see first that the argument in both camps depends on a distinction between an older form of national loyalty and a newer one. Durham distinguishes between the older loyalty of the French Canadians before and just after the conquest, and the new form typical in the province by the 1830s. The revisionists distinguish between the patriotism of pre-liberal societies and the nationalism that appears on the world scene shortly after the beginnings of the modern period. Durham deplores the new nationality; the revisionists are determined to applaud it. Nevertheless it is clear that they are observing the same phenomenon. As we shall see, both seem to suggest that what characterizes the new nationality above all is that it is perceived by members of the collectivity as their choice; it is seen as a function of men's decision to remain associated with the collectivity or to organize politically on the basis of the collectivity. The quarrel, then, is between those who argue that the new form of nationality means that nationalist differences are likely to persist and that they must be accommodated – and Durham, who argues that exactly because nationality has this new form, assimilation is more necessary and more likely.

Charles Taylor presents the distinction between the older nationality and the newer by arguing that for all "emancipated men," meaning men of the modern period, the "political and other structures within which men are set have no inherent value." Political structures once had such value, but no longer. "They are no longer seen as commanding allegiance because, say, they represent the hierarchical order of things, or the chain of being. They are only instruments set up by men to accomplish their purposes."[7] The older form of national loyalty rendered a man subject to the "hierarchical order of things" – a ruler, deity, or natural law that could overrule the impulses and interests of the individual. Such a loyalty, we may suppose, was at once the ground or foundation of society, and the end for which it existed. The new nationality, in contrast, is subject to the individual, a means for the gratification of his impulses and interests, or perhaps one among those interests. David Cameron puts it this way: "Reliance on cultural association" is part of the "good life" for many Canadians.[8] It appears that for both Taylor and Cameron, nationality, "cultural association," is perceived by many to be one of the human goods – comparable to material security and acquisition of possessions.

Many observers of Quebec see a difference between the older and newer allegiance. Marcel Rioux, for example, speaks of three Québécois ideologies, two deserving to be called nationalist. The first was the quiet ideology of "conservation" of the years from 1840 to the end of the Second World War; the second, the ideology of "confrontation and catching up," which Rioux associates with the writings of Pierre Elliott Trudeau and the colleagues who joined him in the federal government. The third, the ideology that emerged in the 1960s, he describes as the "affirmation of Quebec society by development and by participation."[9] The first and third ideologies are both nationalist, in Rioux's description; both are attempts to preserve something distinctively Québécois. But it is a large part of his argument to make the difference between them clear. He describes the aim of the second-period ideologists as the rejection of the "dogmas" of the first period, and he argues that their efforts were largely successful; Quebec was changed in a fundamental way by the efforts of those universalists.[10] He concludes that in the 1950s, the old Québécois way of life was destroyed. The third ideology, then, is new; it is the "negation of the negation represented by the second ideology"; it is both similar and yet in an important way utterly different from the first.[11]

Ormsby argues that French Canada has been "transformed," has "evolved," but is as distinctly different as ever. James de Wilde holds that the "traditional nationalism of French Canada has now almost vanished" and has been replaced by a nationalism that "accepts the logic of social and economic modernization."[12] For these authors Quebec is no longer a projection of the collectivity of the past, la nation canadienne, La Laurentie. And yet it is still recognizably Québécois, le Québec qui se fait. The distinction makes it easier to express appreciation of the threat of assimilation while at the same time voicing hopes for a continuing identity. The old nationality has been extinguished; the new is in the making. Rioux, for example, speaks of the "State of Quebec" as "the only collective instrument that the French Canadians possess." "For French Canada as a whole it's a lost cause sooner or later; the steam roller of English-speaking North American culture will soon leave nothing but a few remnants."[13] Claude Morin speaks of the "increased, many-faceted competition among the various cultures" in the world of the future, which will see only the most vigorous cultures survive. Obtaining the institutions of an independent nation will give Quebec a better chance in this competition.[14] Such a position seems sharply at variance with Burroughs's suggestion that "knowledge concerning cultural differences" will bridge all differences – a simplistic attitude, surely, for if good will and "knowledge" fail to gratify nationalist demands, what is left but to suppose that the French are complaining too much about very little?[15] Nevertheless, at bottom, separatists and multiculturalists, French speaking and English, share a common assumption, and it is this that concerns us here: they hope to save the distinctiveness of a collectivity within Canada, or on the continent, in a world that is daily growing more homogeneous, while at the same time enabling the fullest economic and political development of that collectivity. And they believe that this can perhaps be done by that new form of national loyalty.

Even those of the homogenizing tendency of socialist ideology express this hope. Rioux writes:

It is true that a universalist consciousness is being born and that men everywhere share the same hopes and fears regarding the effects of expanding economic and technological patterns of change on their society. It is not less true that, at the emotional level, the old collective solidarities, by a kind of compensational effect, are becoming once more the place where men secure the roots of their daily life. That these tendencies bring man at the same time towards a universal consciousness and a strong awareness of his own kind is a contradiction in appearance only.[16]

He suggests that because Quebec is starting from a less advanced economic position, it may avoid the mistakes and stages that more developed nations are undergoing and thus benefit in terms of social evelution.[17] But the implication is that indeed all nations move toward "universal consciousness"; Quebec's distinction will be to arrive beforehand. Léon Dion appears to suggest something similar. Disadvantaged groups, Quebec among them, he says, see the future form of political institutions more clearly than the well off.[18] Again the implication is that the new consciousness dawning in Quebec will not differ from that attained by other repressed peoples when they achieve freedom; but it will dawn in Quebec before it does in English Canada. Rioux and Dion start with the supposition that Quebec is underdeveloped; for McRoberts and Posgate suggest the puzzle is exactly that nationalist sentiments have persisted in a society that is already modern and developed. But again, underlying, is the suggestion that in the world now there is a form of nationality immune to the forces of assimilation.

In the revisionist argument what characterizes this new form of national loyalty above all is that it reflects individual preference. The old appeared natural, like life itself. The new is chosen, because it is seen as advantageous. So McRoberts and Posgate suggest that it may be possible to explain the persistence of nationalist identification in Quebec during the years of rapid economic and political change by supposing that nationalism was fostered by members of a new middle-class, trained in the social sciences and in administrative skills, who had committed themselves to nationalism in order to strengthen provincial claims vis à vis the federal government and to build a provincial system of government services, in this way securing employment and careers for themselves.[19] They advance the argument without themselves embracing it, citing several authors in support, notably Albert Breton: "Breton and others seem to be satisfied that the new middle-class attraction to Quebec nationalism was based purely on this ability to legitimize class aspirations."[20] The similarity between this "new middle class thesis," and Durham's argument is obvious. It is true that Durham sees the political leaders of Lower Canada as using nationalist appeals for political ends, such as liberal justice and party victory, whereas the new middle-class theory supposes that nationality was used for chiefly economic and social ends. Durham, moreover, worries that nationalism will be the means to support one-party government, while the new middle-class theorists argue that the emergence of that class led to increased political contestation in the province. The parallel between the politics of the 1830s and the 1960s – which Rioux for one notes – cannot be carried too far. But the resemblance between the theories remains; in both cases it is argued that the expression of nationalist identification continues because ambitious men find it furthers their personal objective. Nationalist loyalties today are chosen, not given; that is the supposition.

This is Taylor's thesis, too. I do not want to minimize the difference between

Taylor and the theorists just described. Taylor supposes that nationalist sentiments are cherished by all, not merely ambitious elites; and he does not believe
that nationalism is merely a means to other ends; he sees it as a good in itself.
Nevertheless, taking the large view, the resemblance is evident. Taylor sees
nationalism as of, and for, the individual – a matter of choice. And he is
just as clear that nationalist feelings of this kind will not remain private; they
will, must, in his view, require public expression.[21] He argues that because
the "language/culture which defines our identity must be one which can com-
mand our allegiance," that is, because we "have to see it as valuable," the
language must be one "used for the whole gamut of human purposes," and
the culture must reflect the aspects of public life that men value. In the modern world this means that a national culture must reflect the achievements
of modern technology and modern economics.[22] This is the new nationality, as against the one based on the "hierarchical order of things." It in some
way mirrors the values of modern societies everywhere, while at the same
time serving to identity individuals with their own people.

For Kenneth McRae it is elites again that are crucial in preserving ethnic
identity. The political system he describes in *Consociational Democracy*, derived from a study of the multi-party societies of Europe, is proposed as a
remedy for the "fatal feud" in this country. The suggestion is that where
each subculture in the larger society is organized separately, and is represented
at the national level by an elite empowered to work out national accomoda-
tions and policies in co-operation with the other representative elites, it is
possible to maintain ethnic cleavages and preserve the distinctive character
of the subcultures without promoting separatism or contestation.[23] It is central to the scheme that the elite in each subculture appeal to the voters on
the basis of ethnicity. As McRae notes, since the elites must be able to articu-
late subculture interests adequately and must also be able to secure acceptance of the decisions reached at the elite level when they report back to their
voters, it is of the first importance that they maintain close relations with
those they claim to speak for, and this relationship must be based on nationality. "If elite-mass relationships are not cohesive, the whole process of negoti-
ation between the subcultures begins to lose meaning."[24] And for this reason, he goes on, "to the extent that ideological quiescence endangers their
position [the elites can] remobilize their followers by an appeal to the dangers
of dismantling the barriers."[25]

While McRae's argument begins with the idea that nationality is a stubborn
fact, in a sense independent of human desires and will, the scheme he favours
as a means of recognizing this fact requires active elites willing to shore
up ethnic identity. The most hard-headed aspect of the scheme is that it
promises those elites personal rewards, that is, electoral victory, for choosing to press political claims in terms of nationality. In other words, he begins
with the idea that nationality is "out there," and that we must build political

institutions recognizing it, but ends by suggesting that it is dependent on individual choice.

I conclude that running through the literature is the idea that nationality today is unlike the older forms of loyalty because it is the product of men's preference.[26] I will not argue that I have given a sufficient account of nationality; I believe, however, that I have identified a significant argument. On the one hand, we have the revisionist argument that liberal institutions must be modified to accommodate this new national sentiment, and on the other, Durham's belief that since it reflects the experience of injustice and in turn promotes injustice, there can be no place for this national loyalty in a liberal polity. The one side argues that the liberal mainstream has shown "little understanding of cultural diversity" and has "neglected cultural entities," the other that because there will always be political leaders ready to use stirring appeals to tradition, community, and fraternity to boost themselves to power, proposals to institutionalize cultural diversity cannot be allowed.[27] The revisionists claim that the new nationality can be a vehicle for political participation, the mode by which individuals press claims in the political arena, among these claims, the demand for recognition of their heritage. We have to ask whether they have met the mainstream supposition that policies enforcing social heterogeneity may limit the individual's freedoms and detract from liberal rights in ways that – for all their desire to retain something of their nationality – most people would find intolerable.

There is no doubt, for example, that Durham would regard consociational democracy as limiting political freedom in an unacceptable way, since it has no institutionalized guarantee for party opposition within each subculture. He would not be alarmed by the idea of elites appealing to the people, but would certainly oppose the suggestion that it should be done in the name of ethnicity. Ethnic appeals may so easily be made to seem natural and indissoluble; it is all too easy for a political elite claiming the voters' allegiance on that basis to come to seem the only correct, natural, and sole political leadership for that group. In short, Durham would reject consociational democracy as more than likely to promote petty tyrannies.

From studies of something very like "elite accommodation" as it was experienced in Canada during the years of what Rioux calls the "first ideology," the years of "conservation," we might conclude that it is in fact far from admirable. Reginald Whitaker describes the "accommodations" of that period as "economic accommodations of class alliances cutting across the two ethnic and linguistic communities," a "fateful tradeoff of mutual elite interests." "Under these circumstances," he says, "Quebec would find it very difficult indeed to develop an indigenous bourgeoisie, so necessary for autonomous capitalist development, and would be saddled with internal elites dependent upon the English, and with a vested interest in fostering economic backwardness and political subservience among the mass of the population."[28] His words have the true Durham ring. Even those who would argue that there was something to admire in the old Québécois way of life will admit that preserving it was costly, a cost paid in a growing sense of frustration and humiliation as French Canadians came to see their own political leaders condoning a system in which all too often unqualified men succeeded in the provincial economy solely because they were from an English-speaking background.[29]

At the same time, it has to be said that the studies of European societies that McRae and his colleagues cite as instances of consociational democracy suggest that nothing so repressive has developed in those countries. Rather, as McRae notes, there has been a tendency for the distinct character of the subcultures to break down.[30] But following Durham's analysis, we would see this as a hopeful sign, suggesting that those countries had come to admit fruitful competition among political parties in conditions of political freedom, with the result that assimilation of a peaceful nature was under way. The fact that even in these systems, apparently designed to promote differences, the barriers are coming down goes far to suggest the worth of Durham's analysis.[31]

That institutionalizing ethnicity promotes injustice is the heart of Durham's case. But his argument suggests as well that the new nationality – for all the sound and fury – is no less prone to assimilation than the old. He would most certainly argue that a nationality that concerns itself with the goals valued by all or most men in this era – with technology and modern economics, to use Taylor's examples – must be described as the expression of assimilated individuals. Taylor argues that nationality defines the individual. He admits, nevertheless, that where it is one among many political goals, it has lost its character as absolute. He argues, too, that the individual shapes the nationality, adapting it to embody international values, so that he can be proud of it and so that it stands well against other backgrounds. Durham would agree that the new nationality has lost its absolute character. He would say, too, that those who believe that men today chose and define nationality are correct. But he would also say that these authors are mistaken if they think that they are describing anything other than completely assimilated individuals. He argues, as we have seen, that the new nationality is an index of the fact of assimilation.

We would conclude from Durham's analysis that to suppose that differences of language or origin or religion are significant cleavages in modern society, as significant as the quarrel between the religious parties of seventeenth-century England, or the difference between the French and English in Quebec in 1759, is a measure of our ignorance of the dimension of those past differences, and the character of the ways of life we have relinquished. It is exactly because Durham sees that nationality – the new form – is of, for, the individual, that he believes assimilation is inevitable. It is because he thinks that nationality in a modern society will have this character that he can maintain that his proposal to hasten assimilation is justified. The question for Durham would be whether this assimilation will bring peaceful co-operation or the growth of national quarrels in new forms, stirring up discrimination in a new way.

All this is not to say that Durham believed that differences between peoples would be completely erased. As he noted in the case of Louisiana, an assimilated people may long retain their language. Roebuck's stand is stronger, and no less compatible with the mainstream. Although he was convinced that the French Canadians were already assimilated to the continental way of life, he nevertheless expected them to keep their language indefinitely. Certainly the mainstream argument suggests that habits of friendship will remain, as will private ethnic and nationalist associations, including schools, churches, and community cultural institutions; so also will memories of the old way of life and all shared experiences, including the experience of adapting to a new way of life.

It could be argued that the insistence on recognition in law of national and ethnic differences will break down the distinction between public and private that is central to liberalism; it will devalue the private, and so work to make those private national and ethnic associations not more but less secure, less protected and less valued in modern society. It may be that the revisionists' argument threatens the continuing existence of habits and associations derived from the old distinctive ways of life, as the mainstream prescription does not.

Durham rejected the idea of a separate French-Canadian nation. But he believed that the several colonies of British North America could come together some day to form a new "national existence," a "counterbalance" on the continent to the United States. It is clear that his argument for a separate British North America could be used today, not only to justify the separation of Quebec from Canada, but to give us a realistic picture of what the new French-Canadian nation would be like. He did not argue for autonomy for French Canada in 1839, because he feared the escalation of national hostilities. We do not fear that today. We can confidently say that a new Nation Canadienne would be tolerant, free, and just, in the way that the province on the banks of the St Lawrence now is tolerant, free, and just. What Durham's argument forces on us is the idea that exactly because it rejected intolerance and injustice, the new nation would be like other modern liberal states in all important respects.

He suggests that the federation of the British colonies would consist of a population virtually identical in political habits, customs, and "manners" with the people of the United States. It is true that many people since have found it worthwhile to live in that federation, although it has, surely, precisely the national character he predicted. Modern states do not allow for all human possibilities, or all desireable ways of life; nevertheless, because they promise freedom, opportunity, and liberal justice, people gladly give them their allegiance. A new Nation Canadienne would be loved, as the province today is loved, as Canada is loved, first and foremost for its adherence to principles that are universally acclaimed and that are enshrined in the constitutions of liberal governments everywhere. Our sense of the familar and our pleasure in a shared life play a part in our attachment to country, but what secures loyalty above all is the belief that our nation is striving for justice. The importance of the mainstream analysis is that it tells us that justice is threatened when a particular way of life is privileged.

It is far from clear that the liberal tradition needs revising in order to account for the continuation of nationalist movements in the modern world. It is even less clear that it could be revised so as to provide for both liberal justice and the recognition of collectivities in law. Durham's insights, grounded in a thorough understanding of the British liberal tradition, which still in a broad sense describes modern nations, certainly those on this continent, may well be true for the foreseeable future.

Notes

PREFACE

1 Gerald Craig, "Introduction," in Craig (ed.), *Lord Durham's Report: An Abridgement of Report on the Affairs of British North America by Lord Durham* (Toronto: McClelland and Stewart, Carleton Library 1968), x.
2 Ged Martin, *The Durham Report and British Policy* (Cambridge: Cambridge University Press 1972), 69.
3 "Whatsoever is lawful in the commonwealth cannot be prohibited by the magistrate in the church" (Locke, *A Letter Concerning Toleration* [Indianapolis: Bobbs-Merrill, Library of Liberal Arts 1950], 40). For the term "outward court," see p. 46.
4 See, for example, William Mathie, "Political Community and the Canadian Experience: Reflections on Nationalism, Federalism and Unity," *Canadian Journal of Political Science,* 12 (March 1979): 8.
5 Marcel Rioux refers to French Canada as "the first colony" and argues that the French Canadians are "without a doubt, among the oldest colonized peoples in the world, if not *the* oldest" (*Quebec in Question*, translated by James Boake [Toronto: Lorimer 1971], 3).

CHAPTER ONE

1 C.P. Lucas (ed.), *Lord Durham's Report on the Affairs of British North America* (Oxford: Clarendon Press 1912, 3 vols), 2: 63, 64. Gerald Craig (ed.), *Lord Durham's Report: An Abridgement of Report on the Affairs of British North America by Lord Durham* (Toronto: McClelland and Stewart, Carleton Library 1968), 47. All references to the Report are made first to the text reproduced in full in volume two of the Lucas edition, cited throughout as *Report*, and then where possible to the Craig edition. Volume one of the Lucas edition consists of Lucas's introduction, and volume three of relevant dispatches, reports, and Charles Buller's

Sketch of Lord Durham's Mission to Canada in 1838. The Lucas edition was reprinted by Augustus M. Kelley in 1970. The Report was first published in London in 1839 by Ridgways, as *Report and Despatches of the Earl of Durham, Her Majesty's High Commissioner and Governor-General of British North America.*

2 *Report*, 70, 307; Craig edition, 50, 159.

3 *Report*, 288; Craig edition, 146.

4 *Report*, 16; Craig edition, 22.

5 William Ormsby, "Lord Durham and the Assimilation of French Canada," in Norman Penlington (ed.), *On Canada, Essays in Honour of Frank H. Underhill* (Toronto: University of Toronto Press 1971), 37.

6 Craig, "Introduction," in Craig (ed.), *Lord Durham's Report*, x.

7 Chester New, *Lord Durham: A Biography of John George Lambton, First Earl of Durham* (Oxford: Clarendon Press 1929), 497. Reviewing the 1968 edition of New's book, Peter Burroughs said, "Although forty years have elapsed, our view of Lord Durham corresponds very closely to the portrait drawn by Chester New in his celebrated biography" (*Canadian Historical Review* 52 [1971]: 190).

8 R. MacGregor Dawson, *The Government of Canada*, 4th ed., revised by Norman Ward (Toronto: University of Toronto Press 1963), 10.

9 A.L. Burt, *The Evolution of the British Empire and Commonwealth from the American Revolution* (Boston: D.C. Heath 1956), 261.

10 Peter Burroughs, *The Canadian Crisis and British Colonial Policy, 1828–1841* (Toronto: Macmillan 1972), 1, 103.

11 Mason Wade, *The French Canadians, 1760–1967*, vol. 1 (Toronto: Macmillan 1968), 184–214.

12 Ormsby, "Lord Durham and the Assimilation of French Canada," 37. See also Ormsby (ed.), *Crisis in the Canadas, 1838–1839: The Grey Journals and Letters* (Toronto: Macmillan 1964), 10.

13 Burroughs, *The Canadian Crisis and British Colonial Policy*, 5.

14 Wade, *The French Canadians*, 198.

15 Craig, "Introduction," in Craig (ed.), *Lord Durham's Report*, x. Other authors using this approach will be discussed below and in chapters two and five. Some not mentioned there can be noted. Duncan McArthur, "Lord Durham and the Union of the Canadas," in Adam Shortt and Arthur G. Doughty (eds), *Canada and Its Provinces: A History of the Canadian People and Their Institutions by One Hundred Associates* (Toronto: Publishers' Association of Canada 1913). McArthur strikes exactly the note of most later Canadian commentators: "The vulnerable point in Lord Durham's Report was his treatment of nationalism" (405). W.P.M. Kennedy, *The Constitution of Canada, 1534–1937: An Introduction to Its Development, Law and Custom* (New York: Russell and Russell 1922). J.L. Morison, "The Mission of the Earl of Durham," in J. Holland Rose, A.P. Newton, E.A. Benians, and W.P.M. Kennedy (eds), *The Cambridge History of the British Empire*, vol. 6 (Cambridge: Cambridge University Press 1930).

R.G. Trotter, *The British Empire-Commonwealth: A Study in Political Evolution* (Toronto: Macmillan 1932). Alexander Brady, *Democracy in the Dominions: A Comparative Study of Institutions* (Toronto: University of Toronto Press 1947). Chester New, George W. Brown, Chester Martin, and D.C. Harvey, in articles in the issue of the *Canadian Historical Review* 20 (1939), celebrating the 100th anniversary of the publication of the Report. J.M.S. Careless, *The Union of the Canadas: The Growth of Canadian Institutions, 1841–1857* (Toronto: McClelland and Stewart 1967). George Woodcock, *Who Killed the British Empire? An Inquest* (London: Jonathan Cape 1974). Authors with a different perspective – in particular the French-Canadian writers whose view is not at all in line with the English Canadians – will receive their due in the next chapter.

16 Martin undertakes to deflate Durham's reputation generally, and the importance of the proposal for "responsible government" in particular, by arguing that Durham's ideas were not original, and that they had little effect on subsequent events. He provides no analysis of the text (*The Durham Report and British Policy* [Cambridge: Cambridge University Press 1972], 69). William Thomas, in *The Philosophic Radicals: Nine Studies in Theory and Practice, 1817–1841* (Oxford: Clarendon Press 1979), is even more anxious to reveal Durham as a figure of no account and pays even less attention to the text.

17 For this usage see Kenneth McRae, "The Plural Society and the Western Political Tradition," *Canadian Journal of Political Science* 12 (1979).

18 Kenneth McRoberts and Dale Posgate, *Quebec, Social Change and Political Crisis* (Toronto: McClelland and Stewart 1980), 144. See also the first chapter in the 1976 edition of this book, "The Quebec 'Problem.'" Where McRoberts and Posgate have occasion to refer to Durham – in a brief historical survey – they follow the customary evaluation and refer to his "racial and imperialistic biases" (see 31 in the 1980 edition).

19 David Cameron, *Nationalism, Self-Determination and the Quebec Question* (Toronto: Macmillan 1974), 1, 2.

20 Gordon Means, "Human Rights and the Rights of Ethnic Groups – A Commentary," *International Studies Notes* 1 (1974): 12.

21 New, *Lord Durham*, 506. And see H.W. McCready's introduction to the abridged edition of New's biography, *Lord Durham's Mission to Canada: An Abridgement of Lord Durham, Biography of John George Lambton, First Earl of Durham by Chester New* (Toronto: McClelland and Stewart, Carleton Library 1963), xi.

22 W.P. Morrell, *British Colonial Policy in the Mid-Victorian Age* (Oxford: Clarendon Press 1963), 471.

23 Craig "Introduction," in Craig (ed.), *Lord Durham's Report*, xi.

24 Nicholas Mansergh, *The Commonwealth Experience* (London: Weidenfield and Nicolson 1969), 30.

25 Kenneth McNaught, *The Pelican History of Canada*, updated edition (Harmondsworth: Penguin Books 1982), 94.

26 W.L. Morton, *The Kingdom of Canada: A General History from Earliest Times*,

2nd ed. (Toronto: McClelland and Stewart 1968), 253.

27 *Report*, 293; Craig edition, 149. See Ramsay Cook on this passage in *Canada and the French Canadian Question* (Toronto: Macmillan 1966), 82, 83: "Lord Durham's prediction was a fairly accurate one."

28 "Much as they struggle against it, it is obvious that the process of assimilation is already commencing" (*Report*, 295; Craig edition, 151). See, for example, 24, where Durham suggests that, much as they might regret the loss of their nationality, the mass of the people were ready to relinquish the laws that maintained it. "There is every reason to believe that a great number of the peasants who fought at St. Denis and St. Charles, imagined that the principal result of success would be the overthrow of tithes and feudal burthens." A full discussion must be postponed until chapter seven.

29 See references in note 1, above.

30 *Report*, 63–72; Craig edition, 47–51.

31 *Report*, 34, 36, 63; Craig edition, 30, 32, 46.

32 *Report* 35–7; Craig edition, 31, 32.

33 *Report*, 288; Craig edition, 145.

34 John Arthur Roebuck was one. His views are discussed in chapters six and seven.

35 *Report*, 21, 22; Craig edition, 25, 26.

36 *Report*, 58; Craig edition, 43. It might be noted that Durham did not propose to eradicate all traces of the French-Canadian way of life. In fact, he speaks of an "amalgamation" of French and English laws, and recommended policies of bilingualism (*Report*, 296, 301, 302; Craig edition, 151, 155, 156). What the commentators take to be deep-seated cultural differences, and proof that individuals can embrace both modernity and "particularism," many nineteenth-century liberals, as we shall see, would regard as no more than pleasant variations on the dominant liberal theme. On "cultural" differences today, see Howard Brotz, "Multiculturalism in Canada: A Muddle," *Canadian Public Policy* 6 (1980).

37 See *Report*, 27; Craig edition, 27, where Durham refers to the institutions of New France as "central ... unimproving and repressive."

38 *Report*, 75–6; Craig edition, 54.

39 *Report*, 73, 79, 279; Craig edition, 53, 56, 140.

40 One great consequence of the Glorious Revolution was the peaceful alternation of parties in power – what Durham refers to as the merely "ordinary animosities of party in a free country" (*Report*, 299; Craig edition, 154). We see it today as the defining characteristic of a liberal democracy. For an understanding of the significance of 1688 that appears to agree exactly with Durham's, see Harvey C. Mansfield Jr, "Party Government and the Settlement of 1688," *American Political Science Review* 58 (1964).

CHAPTER TWO

1 Mason Wade, *The French Canadians 1760–1967*, vol. 1 (Toronto: Macmillan

1968), 210. Compare William Ormsby,*The Emergence of the Federal Concept in Canada, 1839–1845* (Toronto: University of Toronto Press 1969), 4; and Ormsby, "Lord Durham and the Assimilation of Frank Canada," in Norman Penlington (ed.), *On Canada: Essays in Honour of Frank H. Underhill* (Toronto: University of Toronto Press 1971), 37.

2   R. MacGregor Dawson, *The Government of Canada*, 4th ed., revised by Norman Ward (Toronto: University of Toronto Press 1963), 10.

3   L'Abbé Arthur Maheux, "Durham et la Nationalité Canadienne-Française" in *Report of the Canadian Historical Association* (1945), 23. In the discussion following the reading of this paper, Chester New remarked that Durham's recommendation was "entirely wrong." "Durham was too much of an Anglo-Saxon," he commented, "being all for progress." There were remarks by others of the same character.

4   Ged Martin, *The Durham Report and British Policy* (Cambridge: Cambridge University Press 1972) 51, 52. Compare J.R.M. Butler, "Colonial Self-Government, 1838–1852," in J. Holland Rose, A.P. Newton, E.A. Bemans (eds), *The Cambridge History of the British Empire* (Cambridge: Cambridge University Press) 1940, 3 vols), 2: 360: "Durham's policy of anglicizing the French was never tried in fact; it was too ruthless to be carried through by Englishmen."

5   G.P. de T. Glazebrook, *A History of Canadian Political Thought* (Toronto/Montreal: McClelland and Stewart 1966), 109.

6   Ormsby, *The Emergence of the Federal Concept*, 33.

7   See for example, Pierre Elliott Trudeau, "Some Obstacles to Democracy in Quebec," in Trudeau, *Federalism and the French Canadians* (Toronto: Macmillan 1968); Wade, *The French Canadians*, chapter five, and Ormsby, *The Emergence of the Federal Concept*, chapter two.

8   Donald Smiley, *Canada in Question: Federalism in the Eighties*, 3rd ed. (Toronto: McGraw-Hill Ryerson 1980), 215, 216.

9   Jacques Monet, "French Canada: The Coming of Age,"*Globe and Mail*, November 23, 1981, 10.

10   Kenneth McRae (ed.),"Consociationalism and the Canadian Political System," in McRae (ed.), *Consociational Democracy: Political Accommodation in Segmented Societies* (Toronto: McClelland and Stewart 1974), 255. See also Peter Burroughs, *The Canadian Crisis and British Colonial Policy, 1828–1841* (Toronto: Macmillan 1972), 108.

11   Smiley, *Canada in Question*, 216.

12   James de Wilde, "The Parti Québécois in Power," in Richard Simeon (ed.),*Must Canada Fail?* (Montreal: McGill-Queen's University Press 1977), 20, 21.

13   Ormsby, "Lord Durham and the Assimilation of French Canada," 53.

14   Kenneth McRoberts and Dale Posgate, *Quebec, Social Change and Political Crisis*, rev. ed. (Toronto: McClelland and Stewart 1980), 23. But Donald Creighton strikes a different note. In his exposition of the ideas of the Montreal English

merchants, he nowhere underestimates the part that the Montrealers played in convincing Durham that a legislative union of the Canadas, building a progressive and prosperous commercial nation on British ideas, principles, and political practices, would be preferable to a federal union in which the French would remain unassimilated, obstructive, and no doubt disloyal *(The Commercial Empire of the St. Lawrence, 1760–1850* [Toronto: Ryerson 1937]). See also "The Commercial Class in Canadian Politics," in Creighton, *Towards the Discovery of Canada* (Toronto: Macmillan 1972), and his *Dominion of the North* (Toronto: Macmillan 1957). Although Chester New, Mason Wade, and others note that the Montreal merchants influenced Durham, they make it clear that in their opinion this influence was unfortunate, and that the merchants misled Durham in a regrettable fashion.

15 McRae, "The Plural Society and the Western Political Tradition," *Canadian Journal of Political Science* 12 (1979).

16 Charles Taylor, "Why Do Nations Have to Become States?" in Stanley French (ed.), *Philosophers Look at Confederation* (Montreal: Canadian Philosophical Association 1979).

17 David Cameron, *Nationalism Self-Determination and the Quebec Question* (Toronto: Macmillan 1974), 8.

18 Gerald Craig, "Introduction," in Craig (ed.), *Lord Durham's Report* (Toronto: McClelland and Stewart, Carleton Library 1968), x. Compare Craig, *Upper Canada: The Formative Years, 1784–1841* (Toronto: McClelland and Stewart 1968), 264: "But as an Englishman who rejoiced in the progress of his American cousins Durham fell into the trap of believing that there was only one road into the future: the submerging of all other cultures and outlooks by the dominant Anglo-Saxon way of life."

19 Wade, *The French Canadians*, xvi.

20 *Report*, 14, 16; Craig edition, 21, 22.

21 *Report*, 27.

22 Denis Bertrand and André Lavallée, in Bertrand and Albert Desbiens, *Le Rapport Durham* (Montréal: Les Editions Sainte-Marie 1969), xlviii.

23 Compare *Report*, 307, and especially 71, where Durham speaks of the influences that might have "brought the quarrel to its natural and necessary termination" (Craig edition, 159, 51).

24 Bertrand and Lavallée, in *Le Rapport Durham*, ii.

25 Marcel-Pierre Hamel, *Le Rapport de Durham* (Editions du Québec 1948), 51.

26 See Etienne Parent's argument for "responsible government" in *Le Canadien*, June 19, 1833, reprinted in Jean-Charles Falardeau, *Etienne Parent, 1802–1874: Biographie, textes et bibliographie* (Montréal: Les Editions La Presse 1975). It also appears in Hamel's edition of the Report under the heading, "Retrospective d'Etienne Parent." Another who accepted the logic of Durham's argument at this time was John Neilson, editor of *La Gazette de Québec*. Since Neilson was an ardent supporter of the French nationality in these years, he immediately spoke out

against "responsible government," and on behalf of the existing imperial connection and form of government within Quebec (Monet, *The Last Cannon Shot: A Study of French-Canadian Nationalism, 1837–1850* [Toronto: University of Toronto Press 1969], 27–30). But, to put this in perspective, see Louis-Joseph Papineau's bitter response to the Report in *Histoire de l'insurrection du Canada, en réfutation du Rapport de Lord Durham* (Burlington and Paris: 1839; Quebec: 1968).

27   This article is also printed in Falardeau, *Etienne Parent*. My perspective here is in line with the one suggested by Ramsay Cook: "Parent had evidently fully understood the implication of Durham's predictions," he notes (*Canada and the French-Canadian Question* [Toronto: Macmillan 1966], 90). But see H.D. Forbes, "Etienne Parent, Liberal and Nationalist," a paper prepared for the Canadian Political Science Association Annual Meeting, 1983. Forbes argues that such statements as I have quoted are not central to Parent's liberal point of view, and show him in an atypical, momentarily disheartened mood.

28   Hamel, *Le Rapport de Durham*, 51. See also Jean-Paul Bernard, *Les Rouges, Liberalisme, Nationalisme et Anticléricalisme au Milieux de XIXe Siècle* (Montréal: Les Presses de l'Université du Québec 1971), especially 22; and Monet, *The Last Cannon Shot*, 27.

29   Cook, *Canada and the French-Canadian Question*, 138, 139; and see 131; see also Michel Brunet, "The British Conquest and the *Canadiens*," *Canadian Historical Review* 40 (June 1959). William Ormsby, discussing the institutional factors that in his opinion have promoted the survival of French nationalism, takes care to mention the school of French-Canadian historians who have done the most to cast doubt on the idea that British institutions have promoted la survivance: "As leaders of the nationalist school of French-Canadian historians, Guy Fregault, Maurice Seguin, and Michel Brunet have claimed ... that French-Canadian society was derived of its mercantile bourgeoisie at the conquest and thus, although total assimilation did not take place, the culture of French Canada was capable of only a wretched half-survival. For them, French Canada did not achieve an ultimate victory in the union ... and *la survivance* is more myth than reality" (*The Emergence of the Federal Concept*, 4).

30   Martin, *The Durham Report and British Policy*, 79–84.

31   The connection between revived interest in the Report and the South African crisis is discussed in Richard Garnet, "The Authorship of Lord Durham's Canada Report, "*English Historical Review* 17 (1902). Ronald Hyam describes the politicans' use of the Report during this period in *Elgin and Churchill at the Colonial Office, 1905–1908: The Watershed of Empire* (London: Macmillan 1968). See also Martin, *The Durham Report and British Policy*. Martins's bibliography is a good guide to the authors of this period.

32   H.E. Egerton and W.L. Grant, *Canadian Constitutional Development Shown by Selected Speeches and Despatches* (London: John Murray 1907), vi.

33   C.P. Lucas (ed.), *Lord Durham's Report on the Affairs of British North America (Oxford: Clarendon Press 1912)*, 1: 134, 135.

34 Ibid., 134.
35 Ibid., 280.
36 See Egerton, *A Short History of British Colonial Policy* (London: Methuen 1897), especially 525, 526.
37 Egerton, *The Origin and Growth of Greater Britain: An Introduction to Sir C.P. Lucas' Historical Geography* (Oxford: Clarendon Press 1824; first published, 1902), 179. For a dissenting voice from this period, see F. Bradshaw, *Self-Government in Canada and How It Was Achieved: The Story of Lord Durham's Report* (London: P.S. King 1903), 262: "He wished to secure liberty to French and English alike and to prevent the oppression of either."

CHAPTER THREE

1 Alexis de Tocqueville, *De la Démocratie en Amérique,* tome 1 (Paris: Garnier-Flammarion 1981), 537.
2 *Report,* 289; Craig edition, 146.
3 Tocqueville was in England in 1833, and again in 1835 after the publication of volume one of *De la Démocratie* (see Seymour Drescher, *Tocqueville and England* [Cambridge, MA: Harvard University Press 1964]). Durham's Russian missions took him out of the country just at the time of these visits. Although he could have used the English translation by Henry Reeve, part of which appeared in 1835, it is more likely that Durham read the French. Where Tocqueville refers to "la race Anglaise," for example, Reeve has "the British race," and Durham, "the English race." There are several instances in all where Durham uses the cognate rather than a term from the translation. And note Durham's reference to "a French writer" (*Report,* 91). A comparison of his argument on 90, 91, with Tocqueville's on 540, 541 of *De la Démocratie* shows that beyond doubt Durham is referring to Tocqueville here.
4 Tocqueville, *De la Démocratie,* 1: 539. An invaluable guide to Tocqueville's writings on Canada is Jacques Vallée, *Tocqueville au Bas-Canada* (Montréal: Editions du Jour 1973). I consulted this volume frequently.
5 Drescher, *Tocqueville and England,* 25–8.
6 Tocqueville, *Journey to America,* edited by J.-P. Mayer, (New York: Anchor Books 1971), 162.
7 Tocqueville, *De la Démocratie,* 1: 549. Note Hugh Brogan, "Alexis de Tocqueville and the Liberal Movement," *The Historical Journal* 14 (1971): "[Tocqueville's] pages contain almost nothing on ... nationalism" (298); "He overlooked nationalism altogether. Yet this was the rock on which the liberalism of 1830 and 1848, like so many universal creeds before and since, was to founder" (299). It would seem that Brogan regards only a pluralist position as a statement concerning nationalism.
8 See Edgar McInnis, "A Letter from Alexis de Tocqueville on the Canadian Rebellion of 1837," *Canadian Historical Review* 19 (1938).

9 *Report,* 288; Craig edition, 146.

10 *Report,* 289; Craig edition, 146.

11 Tocqueville, *De la Démocratie,* 1: 67.

12 Ibid., 530.

13 Ibid., 332. Both Durham and Tocqueville in fact use the term much as John Stuart Mill does in his essay, "Civilization," *London and Westminster Review* 25 (1836). Both would have known of this article.

14 *Report,* 211, 183, and see 138, 145, 262; Craig edition, 114, 99, 73, 77, 129.

15 Tocqueville, *De la Démocratie,* 1: 340.

16 *Report,* 37, 38; Craig edition, 33.

17 *Report,* 30, 263, 99; Craig edition, 28, 130, 99.

18 *Report,* 30; Craig edition, 28.

19 *Report,* 30, 28; Craig edition, 28, 27.

20 *Report,* 295; Craig edition, 151.

21 Durham describes language, laws, habits, and customs (*Report,* 29, 267; Craig edition, 49, 132) as influencing the "national character" (68, 288; Craig edition, 49, 146) of a "race." He speaks of "habits" and "sentiments" (170), "institutions and customs" (289; Craig edition, 146), and using the term favoured by previous political thinkers, refers to the public "manners" of English and French: "manners, customs, laws" (38, 289, 303; Craig edition, 33, 146, 157). In short, he believes it is language, laws, and political "manners" that affect "race" and not origin or genetic inheritance.

22 *Report,* 26, 37, 46, 289, 291; Craig edition, 27, 33, 35, 146, 147.

23 *Speeches of the Earl of Durham delivered at Public Meetings in Scotland in 1834,* 8th ed. (London: James Ridgway and Sons 1838), 17. This speech was given in October 1834. See also his speech to his own constituents at Sunderland in 1833, where he says that it had been his object throughout his political career to "endeavour to create some public feeling in the country – some attachment to constitutional principles – in short to induce the people of the country to think for themselves" (*Speeches of the Earl of Durham on Reform of Parliament,* 8th ed. (London: James Ridgway and Sons 1838), 198.

24 Hansard, Series 3 (March 28, 1831), 1014–1134.

25 For Durham's use of "large" in this sense, see *Report,* 20, 301; Craig edition, 25, 155. "Large" programs are opposed to "narrow" or "partial" objects, in one instance to "narrow national prejudices." He means by his praise of "large" programs to approve what Tocqueville would call "enlightened self-interest."

26 See especially, *Report,* 46; Craig edition 36; and Tocqueville, *De la Démocratie,* 1: 64, 99, 115, 537.

27 *Report,* 30, 31; Craig edition, 28.

28 *Report,* 27; Craig edition, 27.

29 Tocqueville, *De la Démocratie,* 1: 388.

30 *Report,* 30; Craig edition, 28.

31 For Durham as mine-owner, and an account of the measures he initiated to alleviate

the poverty of his employees, see Chester New, *Lord Durham: A Biography of John George Lambton, First Earl of Durham* (Oxford: Clarendon Press 1929).

32   See *Report,* 293, 294; Craig edition, 149, 150.

33   Peter Burroughs, *The Canadian Crisis and British Colonial Policy, 1828–1841* (Toronto: Macmillan 1972), 5. Gerald Craig, "Introduction," in Craig (ed.), *Lord Durham's Report* (Toronto: McClelland And Stewart 1963), x.

34   Donald Creighton argues that the first British governors of French Canada – James Murray, Guy Carleton, and Frederick Haldimand – preferred the obedient and pacific French to the aggressive, insubordinate English (*The Commercial Empire of the St. Lawrence, 1760–1850* [Toronto: Ryerson 1956], 39). Of all the American colonies, he says, the French province was the most un-American; astonishingly, in the midst of the American forest it appeared to preserve "the old certainties and the old simplicities." See for illustration, Murray's letter to the Montreal Board of Trade, October 29, 1764, in Adam Shortt and A.G. Doughty (eds), *Documents Relating to the Constitutional History of Canada, 1759–1791* (Ottawa: King's Printer 1907), 167, where he refers to the French as "the best and bravest race upon the Globe." Carleton's admiration of the French is evident in his letters to Shelburne, November 25 and December 24, 1767, in Shortt and Doughty, 196–9, 201–3. Creighton does not list the "old certainties"; presumably they were beliefs that Protestant representatives of a British king could share with Catholics recently loyal to France.

35   "Universal and homogeneous": the phrase is from Alexandre Kojève's essay, "Tyranny and Wisdom" (see Leo Strauss, *On Tyranny*, revised and enlarged [Ithaca, NY: Cornell University Press 1968]). As I have used it here, it will be familiar from George Grant's discussion of the dialogue between Kojève and Strauss in Grant, *Technology and Empire: Perspectives on North America* (Toronto: House of Anansi 1969), and from chapter 6 in Grant's *Lament for a Nation* (Toronto: McClelland and Stewart 1965).

36   *Report,* 267, 268; Craig edition, 132, 133.

37   Tocqueville, *De la Démocratie*, 1: 536. The fact that Durham and Tocqueville saw no difference in national character north and south of the border between British North America and the United States is the more interesting given the arguments of those like Gad Horowitz who suggest that the conservative tendencies of the Loyalist immigration from the United States at the end of the eighteenth century would have marked Canada with a distinctive and "un-American tory ... touch" (see Gad Horowitz, *Canadian Labour in Politics* (Toronto: University of Toronto Press 1968), chapter one.

38   *Report,* 99, 206; Craig edition, 60, 112.

39   *Report,* 212; Craig edition, 114. The entire section runs from 211–18; Craig edition, 113–16. And see 49, 91–2, 114, 184–5, 201, 206, 261–2; Craig edition, 38, 60, 61, 68, 100, 101, 108, 112, 127, 128. John Uhr first drew my attention to these passages in a paper delivered to the graduate students' association in the Department of Political Economy at the University of Toronto in 1978.

Charles Buller draws much the same picture as Durham in his Special Report
on Crown Lands, prepared for Durham (C.P. Lucas, *Lord Durham's Report
on the Affairs of British North America* [Oxford: Clarendon Press 1912],
3: 34-130, esp. 67-9).

40   *Report,* 212; Craig edition, 114.

41   *Report,* 213.

42   Ibid. 212-13, 215-16; Craig edition, 115.

43   *Report,* 206, 216, 261, 331; Craig edition, 112, 115, 128, 173. Compare Tocqueville, *De la Démocratie,* 1: 414.

44   *Report,* 114, 135; Craig edition, 68, 71.

45   *Report,* 204; Craig edition, 110, 111.

46   *Report,* 261; Craig edition, 128.

47   See for example, Thornton Leigh Hunt, *Canada and South Australia: A Commentary on that Part of The Earl of Durham's Report which Relates to the Disposal of Waste Lands and Emigration* (London: A. Gole 1839). This essay consists of three papers, given as public lectures, addressed to Edward Gibbon
Wakefield. The author takes great satisfaction in extolling Wakefield's land-
distribution practices as they had been effected in South Australia. "The system
adopted in South Australia was intended to furnish the most perfect contrast to
the picture exhibited in Canada; and it does so"(32). Durham refers to the Report
of the Select Committee of the House of Commons in 1836, a study of land
disposition in the Australian colonies that contains many references to the United
States and British North America (*Report,* 206). Among those who had contributed to that study were Durham's associates, Edward Gibbon Wakefield and
R.D. Hanson. Hanson, as Durham's Assistant Commissioner of Crown Lands,
was the author of the mission's report on the clergy reserves (Lucas, *Lord
Durham's Report,* 3: 1-6; see Lucas's footnotes, *Report,* 206, 207).

48   See Wakefield's *England and America,* in M.F. Lloyd Pritchard (ed.), *The Col-
lected Works of Edward Gibbon Wakefield* (Glasgow: Collins 1968), and compare, *Report,* 203-6, 219-42; Craig edition, 110-20. Lucas's notes are again
useful. Tocqueville's opinion of these passages in the Durham Report can be
found in his report on Algeria of 1847 (see Vallée, *Tocqueville au Bas-Canada,*
171, 172). In Canada as in Algeria, says Tocqueville, can be found immigrants
who suffer on arrival in the new country from inefficient means of establishing
title to lands and uncultivated wastelands, an absence of capital, and ruined men
who try to obtain property without the means to establish working farms. It was
the proposals in the Durham Report for obtaining title to frontier lands that
interested Tocqueville most in this context.

49   *Report,* 261-2; Craig edition, 127, 128.

50   The phrase is Ged Martin's (*The Durham Report and British Policy* (Cambridge:
Cambridge University Press 1972), 51, 52.

51   *Report,* 71, 307; Craig edition, 51, 59.

52   The tenor of the English party demands in Lower Canada may be judged by

the Address from the Constitutional Association of Montreal, January 1836, reproduced in Appendix A to the *Report* (Lucas, *Lord Durham's Report*, 3: 21–8.

53 *Report*, 301; Craig edition, 155.

54 *Report*, 303; Craig edition, 156.

55 *Report*, 300; Craig edition, 155.

56 *Report*, 301; Craig edition, 155. Compare Tocqueville, *De la Démocratie*, 1: 372n.

57 *Report*, 303; Craig edition, 157.

58 *Report*, 299; Craig edition, 154.

59 See the discussion in chapter two.

60 The Radicals assumed that Durham would represent the Polish cause to the czar. See John Reid's editorial comments in his collection of Durham's speeches (*Sketch of the Political Career of the Earl of Durham* (Glasgow: John Reid 1835), 274, and New, *Lord Durham*, 296. But in fact, Durham was given no such instructions.

61 Foreign Office, "Draft of General Instructions to Lord Durham for guidance in the performance of his duties," Public Record Office, London, FO, 65 200.

62 Craig, "Introduction," in Craig (ed.), *Lord Durham's Report*, x; Burroughs, *The Canadian Crisis*, 1, 5, 103.

63 *Report*, 305, 309; Craig edition, 158, 160.

64 *Report*, 62, 262; Craig edition, 46, 128.

65 *Report*, 58, 59, 61. See also Durham's dispatch of August 9, 1838, to Lord Glenelg (Lucas, *Lord Durham's Report*, 3: 323).

66 See for example, Hansard, 3, 12 (April 13, 1832), 358. The Radicals were also fond of this device. Joseph Hamburger describes the Radicals' threats in *James Mill and the Art of Revolution* (New Haven: Yale University Press 1963).

67 *Report*, 206; Craig edition, 112.

68 *Report*, 262, 332; Craig edition, 128, 129, 172.

69 *Report*, 312; Craig edition, 162. He refers to Adam Smith's passage in *The Wealth of Nations* ascribing colonial dissatisfaction to the lack of scope for ambitious men in dependent colonies.

70 *Report*, 305. Compare 146; Craig edition, 158, 78.

71 Tocqueville, *De la Démocratie*, 1: 330, 331.

72 Ibid., 331.

73 *Report*, 19; Craig edition, 24.

CHAPTER FOUR

1 *Report*, 295; Craig edition, 151.

2 *Report*, 299; Craig edition, 154. His position is exactly in line with Locke's: "I say these have no right to be tolerated by the magistrate that will not own and teach the duty of tolerating all men in matters of mere religion" (*A Letter Concerning Toleration* [Indianapolis: Bobbs-Merrill, Library of Liberal Arts 1950], 51).

3   *Report*, 137 and see 39; Craig edition, 72, 34.

4   *Report*, 140, 308, 325: Craig edition, 74, 159, 169.

5   Durham presented dozens of petitions on behalf of dissenters in March 1834. See also his speeches in the Lords on May 22, 1832, February 21, 1834, and June 9, 1834.

6   *The Examiner*, October 22, 1837, 681.

7   *Report*, 137; Craig edition, 72.

8   *Report*, 138; Craig edition, 73.

9   The Dumont Report, *L'Église du Québec: Un héritage project* (1971), identifies 1840–96 as a period of increasing church influence, and 1896–1940 as the period of church triumph (cited in Abbé Norbert Lacoste, "The Catholic Church in Quebec: Adapting to Change," in Dale C. Thomson [ed.], *Quebec, Society and Politics* [Toronto: McClelland and Stewart 1975]). Pierre Trudeau's comments in "Some Obstacles to Democracy in Quebec," in *Federalism and the French Canadians* (Toronto: Macmillan 1968), are well known. See especially, 103–14. Durham's conviction that this was a modernizing period and that the clergy were prepared to allow the development of a largely non-denominational state shows in his supposition that the priests would support a public school system. (see below, chapter seven). For an admirable discussion of church and state in Quebec in the years after 1840, see Rainer Knopff, "Quebec's 'Holy War' as Regime Politics," *Canadian Journal of Political Science* 12 (1979), esp. 329–31.

10   *Report*, 138; Craig edition, 72.

11   See the letter to Russell Bowlby, July 8, 1837, reproduced in Chester New, *Lord Durham: A Biography of John George Lambton, First Earl of Durham* (Oxford: Clarendon Press 1929), 314.

12   Hansard, Series 3, 21 (March 6, 1834), 1192. Charles Buller is reputed to have put his position this way: "Destroy the Church of England! You must be mad–it is the only thing between us and real religion" (E.M. Wrong's introduction to *Charles Buller and Responsible Government* [Oxford: Clarendon Press 1929], 9, 10).

13   *Report*, 139; Craig edition, 73.

14   *Report*, 308, 325; Craig edition, 159, 169.

15   Alexis de Tocqueville, *De la Démocratie en Amérique* (Paris: Garnier-Flammarion 1981), 1: 401–8.

16   Ibid., 103.

17   *Report*, 212; Craig edition, 114.

18   Tocqueville, *De la Démocratie*, 1: 103.

19   Ibid., 67.

20   Ibid., 103, 104.

21   Ibid., 396–401.

22   Ibid., 392–5. There is one caveat to Tocqueville's suggestion that any religion will serve. He believed that to be effective as the support of freedom, it must be a religion conveying the doctrine of eternal life, that is, a teaching about rewards

and punishments after death.

23   Ibid., 540.

CHAPTER FIVE

1   Chester New, *Lord Durham: A Biography of John George Lambton, First Earl of Durham* (Oxford: Clarendon Press 1929), 495, 496. As Donald Creighton notes in "The Commercial Class in Canadian Politics": "For those who stress responsible government, Lord Durham is a great liberal imperialist, with a regrettable tendency to ruthlessness and bias; for those who neglect union and its implications, the Report is a magnificent treatise on colonial government, marred by certain omissions, inaccuracies, and prejudices" (*Towards the Discovery of Canada* [Toronto: Macmillan 1972], 100).

2.   Reginald Coupland, *The Durham Report: An Abridged Version* (Oxford: Clarendon Press 1945), viii.

3.   See, for example, Durham's description of the political problems of the reformers in Upper Canada, *Report*, 155–9.

4.   See *Report*, 147–51; Craig edition, 78–81.

5   See Durham's discussion of this measure, *Report*, 279; Craig edition, 140.

6   Parent's endorsement of "responsible government" has been mentioned. See chapter two, note 26. For Baldwin's exposition see his letter to Durham of August 28, 1838, and his letter to Lord Glenelg written two years before (*Report on the Public Archives of Canada for the Year 1923* [Ottawa 1924], 326–7).

7   *Report*, 76; Craig edition, 54.

8   *Report*, 278, 279; Craig edition, 138, 139. See also *Report*, 76–82, 150–1, 194, 196, 277–85; Craig edition, 54–8, 80–1, 106, 139–43. Durham did not use the term "responsible government" to refer to the constitutional principle he describes so well. In one passage, for example, he simply speaks of the "true principle of representative government." Until shortly after the publication of the Report, writers used the phrase "responsible government" to refer to any system of which they approved. John Arthur Roebuck, for example, argued that because the people of Upper Canada had wanted "a good, that is, a responsible government," they would seek an elective legislative council (Roebuck, *Existing Difficulties in the Government of the Canadas* [London: C. and W. Reynell 1836], 48). See New, *Lord Durham*, 335–43, for examples of this usage among colonial writers.

9   See Hansard, Series 3, 36 (March 6, 1837), 1295: "That part of the constitution which requires that the Ministers of the Crown shall be responsible to Parliament, and shall be removeable if they do not obtain the confidence of Parliament, is a condition which exists in an imperial legislature and in an imperial legislature only. It is a condition which cannot be carried into effect in a colony … Otherwise … each colony would, in effect, be an independent state." His speech of June 3, 1839, in the Commons, introducing the act to unite the Canadas, and his letter of instruction to Governor Poulett Thomson on "responsible govern-

ment" are even better known (W.P.M. Kennedy [ed.], *Documents of the Canadian Constitution 1759–1915* [Toronto: Oxford University Press 1918], 480, 522–4. Note George Cornewall Lewis's formulation, a great undertaking in the art of definition: "If the government of the dominant country substantially govern the dependency, the representative body cannot substantially govern it; and conversely, if the dependency be substantially governed by the representative body, it cannot be substantially governed by the Government of the dominant country. A self-governing dependency (supposing the dependency not to be virtually independent) is a contradiction in terms" (Lewis, *An Essay on the Government of Dependencies*, edited by C.P. Lucas [Oxford: Clarendon Press 1891; first published 1841]).

10   See for example, John W. Cell's suggestion that Russell was proved right in the long run (*British Colonial Administration in the Mid-Nineteenth Century: The Policy-Making Process* [New Haven: Yale University Press 1978]).

11   *Report*, 282; Craig edition, 141, 142.

12   *Report*, 282, note. And see Lucas's note on the preceding page.

13   Gerald Craig "Introduction," in Craig (ed.), *Lord Durham's Report* (Toronto: McClelland and Stewart 1968), vii.

14   Arthur Berridale Keith is another who suggested that Durham had intented a division of powers (*Responsible Government in the Dominions*, vol. 2 [Oxford: Clarendon Press 1912]). And see J.L. Morison, *British Supremacy and Canadian Self-Government* (Toronto: S.B. Gundy 1919), 244, 245.

15   C.P. Lucas (ed.), *Lord Durham's Report on the Affairs of British North America* (Oxford: Clarendon Press 1912, 3 vols),1: 314.

16   Ibid., 315, 316.

17   Lionel Curtis, *The Commonwealth of Nations* (Toronto: Macmillan 1914). For the influence of the Report on Curtis and others involved in the adventures of empire at this time, see Walter Nimocks, *Milner's Young Men: The "Kindergarten" in Edwardian Imperial Affairs* (Durham, NC: Duke University Press 1968).

18   Coupland, *The Durham Report, An Abridged Version*, vii. Coupland was the third Beit Professor of colonial history at Oxford to write extensively about Durham. Curtis was Beit Professor while writing *The Commonwealth of Nations*. H.E. Egerton had preceded him.

19   Coupland uses "dyarchy," a term originating with Curtis, to refer to this less formalized division-of-powers relationship. Others who elaborate on "dyarchy" or "diarchy" include F.H. Underhill,*The Commonwealth Experience* (Durham, NC: Duke University Press 1956), and D.K. Fieldhouse, *The Colonial Empire: A Comparative Study from the Eighteenth Century* (New York: Delacorte Press 1967).

20   Ged Martin,*The Durham Report and British Policy* (Cambridge: Cambridge University Press 1972), 61.

21   *Report*, 283, 264; Craig edition, 142, 143.

22   *Report*, 282; Craig edition, 142.

23   *Report*, 263, 264; Craig edition, 129, 130.

24 *Report*, 280, 281 and see 194, 277; Craig edition, 141, 139.

25 *Report*, 310, 312, 313, 331–2; Craig edition, 160, 162, 163, 172, 173.

26 For Howe's letters, see Kennedy, *Documents of the Canadian Constitution*, 480–514. Some years later Herman Merivale expressed a position much in line with Howe's: "The Canadian outbreak of 1897 ... directed the thoughts of the more speculative towards the renewal of the older and freer polity of our first American settlements" (from the preface, written in 1861, to *Lectures on Colonization and Colonies, Delivered before the University of Oxford in 1839, 1840 and 1841* [London: Oxford University Press 1928], vi).

27 Lucas, *Lord Durham's Report*, 3: 29. Compare *Report*, 285 and the entire section, 281–5; Craig edition, 143, 141–3.

28 Edward Gibbon Wakefield, "Sir Charles Metcalfe in Canada," first published in 1844, reprinted in E.M. Wrong (ed.), *Charles Buller and Responsible Government* (Oxford: Clarendon Press 1926). Wakefield writes: "For this age and the next it is enough to know that Colonies, built up by our own people, and gifted with our own free institutions, must be bound, alike by the natural feelings and commercial wants of their people, to ourselves and our policy, no less than to our trade" (see 351). Compare *Report*, 310, where Durham entertains the idea of a future separation; Craig edition, 161.

29 Coupland, *The Durham Report*, lxi. And see l'Abbé Arthur Maheux, "Durham et la Nationalité Canadienne-Française," in the *Report of the Canadian Historical Association* (1943), 19–23.

30 Hansard 1, 27 (May 12, 1814). In the same year he attacked the tory ministry for assisting Sicily in its war against Naples, and protested the transfer of Genoa to the rule of the King of Sardinia.

31 Ibid., 1, 29 (November 25, 1814). And see Durham's speech at the Fox anniversary dinner of 1821 where he spoke of the participants at Vienna as a "gang of experienced and notorious poachers on the liberties of mankind" (John Reid, *Sketch of the Political Career of the Earl of Durham* [Glasgow: John Reid and Co. 1835], 98).

32 See Hansard 1, 37 (March 9, 1818), and his speech at the Fox anniversary dinner of 1819 (John Reid, *Sketch*, 72).

33 See New, *Lord Durham*, chapter x, "Belgium."

34 Taylor, "Why Do Nations Have to Become States," in Stanley G. French (ed.), *Philosophers Look at Confederation* (Montreal: Canadian Philosophical Association 1979), 21.

35 "If England continues to be inspired by what Lord Durham taught so well, then as Great Britain has grown into Greater Britain, so Greater Britain will grow into Greatest Britain" (Lucas, *Lord Durham's Report*, 1: 317).

36 Peter Burroughs, *Canadian Historical Review* 52 (June, 1971). It is not only a matter of changing attitudes in the recent generation. The historians have also revised their assessment of the way that empire was viewed in the past. And this, too, has had its effect on opinions of the Report. At the turn of the century,

Durham and his associates were valued so highly in part because they were believed to have been more or less alone in their time in defending the idea of Greater Britain. Charles Buller had encouraged such a view by arguing, for example, that Durham, "alone in his day rightly appreciated the worth of our colonial empire" (*Sketch of Lord Durham's Mission to Canada* in Lucas, *Lord Durham's Report*, 1 : 376). But today it is usually said that Durham and his colleagues were not unique and that many Englishmen of that period held staunchly to the idea of empire (see Burroughs, *The Canadian Crisis and British Colonial Policy* [Toronto: Macmillan 1972], 1, 2). For a fuller story of this revised view of past opinions, see the bibliographic essays in Robin Winks (ed.), *The Historiography of the British Empire-Commonwealth* (Durham, NC: Duke University Press 1966), or the first chapter of C.C. Eldridge, *England's Mission: The Imperial Idea in the Age of Gladstone and Disraeli, 1868–1880* (London: Macmillan 1973). If Durham shines less, then, it is first because the idea of empire ascribed to him is perceived as passé or offensive, and then – strangely – because he and his associates are no longer seen as seminal.

CHAPTER SIX

1   See Durham's use of the term (*Report*, 148; Craig edition, 79).

2   *Report*, 286, Craig edition, 144.

3   *Report*, 287; Craig edition, 145. Gordon T. Stewart (*The Origins of Canadian Politics: A Comparative Approach* [Vancouver: University of British Columbia Press 1986]) is one historian who has paid close attention to these passages.

4   *Report*, 84, 81; Craig edition, 60, 58.

5   *Report*, 155; Craig edition, 84.

6   Hansard, Series 3, 8 (October 7, 1831), 320.

7   R.L. Schuyler, *British Constitutional History since 1832* (Princeton: Anvil Books 1957), 114, 115.

8   J.A.R. Marriott argues, in *England since Waterloo* (New York: G.P. Putnam's Sons 1922), that Grey and his ministers did indeed believe that their efforts at the time of the Reform Bill would not alter the essential features of the British constitution. "The changes of 1867 and 1884 ... implicit in the earlier revolution ... were ... neither foreseen nor intended by Lord Grey and his colleagues ... Neither then nor later had the Whigs any intention of satisfying democratic aspirations" (see 101). He does add that their views may have been characterized by a surprising lack of foresight. G.M. Trevelyan, however, takes the view that the long-term consequences of the Reform Bill, foreseen or unforeseen, should in some sense redound to the credit of the whigs (*British History in the Nineteenth Century (1782–1901)* [London: Longman's Green 1922], 225). When Chester New refers to the Durham Report as "the charter of Canadian democracy," he surely betrays Trevelyan's influence (*Lord Durham: A Biography of John George Lambton, First Earl of Durham* [Oxford: Clarendon Press 1929], 190).

9 Hansard, 3, 3 (March 28, 1831), 1028–9.
10 Hugh Brogan, "Alexis de Tocqueville and the Liberal Movement," *The Historical Journal* 14 (1971): 290.
11 *Report,* 73, 79, 279; Craig edition, 53, 56, 140.
12 *Report,* 277, 278; Craig edition, 139.
13 Only for a comparatively short period in the mid- and late-nineteenth century were the popular houses, in Britain and in the colonies, really able to humble the executive branch and bring ministers to account by making and unmaking governments (see Thomas Hockin, "Flexible and Structured Parliamentarism: From 1848 to Contemporary Party Government," *Journal on Canadian Studies* 14, Special Issue on Responsible Government [1979], and other articles in this issue). Parliamentary systems after that reverted to the strong executive that Durham regarded as the norm. According to Tom Truman, "All the conventions of cabinet government promote a cabinet-solidarity-loyalty to the government and its leaders, and secrecy in relation to public opinion, and this is extended down through the ranks of the government party ... by the twin spirits of partisanship and ambition." It is a system, he goes on, "strong enough to withstand very great public pressure" (Truman, "A Critique of Seymour M. Lipset's Article, 'Value Differences, Absolute or Relative: The English-Speaking Democracies,'" *Canadian Journal of Political Science* 4 [1971]: 511).
14 *Speeches of the Earl of Durham, Delivered at Public Meetings in Scotland in 1834,* 8th ed. (London: Ridgway 1838), 18–19. And see the speech he delivered at Newcastle on the same tour in November (*Speeches of the Earl of Durham in Scotland,* 94).
15 In the Parliament of 1830, the Philosophical Radicals numbered about 12, while the total number of radicals of various colours in this Parliament – followers of O'Connell, Cobbett, Attwood – is placed somewhere between 50 and 100 (Joseph Hamburger, *Intellectuals in Politics: John Stuart Mill and the Philosophic Radicals* [New Haven: Yale University Press 1965], 115). It is sometimes argued that the Philosophical Radicals represented and claimed to represent, not the "people," meaning the majority of the populace, but the middle classes only. See, for example, William Thomas, "James Mill's Politics: The Essay on Government and the Movement for Reform," *The Historical Journal* 12 (1969), and the rejoinder by Wendell Robert Carr, "James Mill's Politics Reconsidered: Parliamentary Reform and the Triumph of Truth," *The Historical Journal* 14 (1971). Hamburger gives the background to this controversy in *Intellectuals in Politics,* 45–53. From my own study of the documents, I am persuaded, with Hamburger, that it is correct to call the Philosophical Radicals majoritarian democrats. This is most certainly true with respect to their representation of Canadian affairs.
16 For the history of Durham's relations with the Radicals, see Hamburger's *Intellectuals in Politics.* I am deeply indebted to Professor Hamburger for my understanting of the politics and personalities of the period. However, Hamburger

suggests that the association between Durham and the Radicals foundered in the end on simple political differences, and on the parliamentary difficulties the Radicals suffered as a minority party, whereas I am convinced that the differences were always on the level of political philosophy. How could the Radicals have possibly supported a man who continued to argue for the prerogatives of the crown, the "honours" of the upper classes, and government by King, Lords, and Commons?

17 Roebuck gives an account of his interview with Durham in *The Colonies of England: A Plan for the Government of Some Portion of Our Colonial Possessions* (London: John W. Parker 1849), 190. At this time, Roebuck prepared a memorandum at Durham's request, and it is this memorandum that Durham showed to Canadian leaders in summer 1838. It is reproduced in *Colonies of England.* Roebuck's opinion of Durham can be seen in a note on 209: "Lord Durham was about as capable of understanding these suggestions as I am of reading Cherokee, of which I do not understand the letters."

18 See William Ormsby, *The Emergence of the Federal Concept in Canada* (Toronto: University of Toronto Press 1969), 19, 20, 39, and notes.

19 Bentham, "Plan of Parliamentary Reform," in *The Works of Jeremy Bentham,* edited by John Bowring (New York: Russell and Russell 1962) 3: 527–8.

20 James Mill, "The State of the Nation," *London Review* 1 (April 1835): 14.

21 See, for example, John Arthur Roebuck's description of the Radicals as a party "of the people" in his letter to Louis-Joseph Papineau in September 1836 (Public Archives of Canada, Roebuck Papers, vol. 2, no. XI). John Stuart Mill reviews Radical hopes for a realignment of the parties and the formation of a new majority party in "Reorganization of the Reform Party," *London and Westminster Review* 32 (1839). From the beginning, the disciples had shaped and sharpened Benthamite teachings to suit the needs of parliamentarians and journalists. See chapter II of Hamburger's *Intellectuals in Politics.* Hamburger tells the complete story of Radical frustrations in this decade.

22 Charles Buller, *On the Necessity of a Radical Reform* (London: Ridgway 1831), 9, 13.

23 Bentham, "Plan of Parliamentary Reform," 450.

24 James Mill, "Essay on Government," in *Essays on Government, Jurisprudence, Liberty of the Press and Law of Nations* (New York: Augustus M. Kelly 1967), 15.

25 Roebuck suggests an elective executive council in *Existing Difficulties in the Government of the Canadas* (London: C. and W. Reynell 1836). Compare, *Report,* 279: "An elective executive council would not only be utterly inconsistent with monarchical government, but would really, under the nominal authority of the Crown, deprive the community of one of the great advantages of an hereditary monarchy."

26 Henry Samuel Chapman, "What is the Result of the Elections. Fully Answered," *Daily Advertiser* (Montreal), December 8, 1834.

27 See, for example, Roebuck, *The Colonies of England,* 201.

28 See Hansard, 3, 36 (January 31, 1837), and Roebuck's description of the party situation in England in his letter to Papineau of September 1836.

29 Roebuck spoke at the bar of the Commons and Lords during the debates in January and February, 1838, on the Canadian rebellions; he wrote to the prime minister, Melbourne, offering to go to Canada as special emissary; and he founded a newspaper, the *Canadian Portfolio,* to present the rebel cause sympathetically to the British people. There were five inflammatory issues of the *Portfolio* before funds dried up.

30 See Janet Ajzenstat, "Collectivity and Individual Right in 'Mainstream' Liberalism: John Arthur Roebuck and the *Patriotes,"* *Journal of Canadian Studies* 19 (Fall 1984).

31 See, for example, Roebuck, *Existing Difficulties,* 25: "It so happens that the interests of the inhabitants or the townships and of the seigneuries, are, in fact, identical. Both portions of the population are purely agricultural, and the circumstances affecting their welfare ... are common to both."

32 Hansard, 3, 26 (March 9, 1835), 670. Colin Pearce has drawn my attention to Egerton Ryerson's championing of Durham's "responsible government" against Roebuck's "government purely democratic" in an editorial in the *Christian Guardian* of June 5, 1839: "Now does Lord Durham propose 'a government democratic'? No! Does he propose to abolish one branch of the Government? No!"

33 Hansard, 3, 36 (March 6, 1837), 1310. Durham responds to the charge that there were English and Americans with the revolutionaries in the Report (see 17–20).

34 See, for example, Roebuck in Hansard, 3, 22 (April 15, 1834), 780–1, 785, 817; and Hansard, 3, 37 (April 14, 1837), 1213–14; Hansard 3, 40 (January 22, 1838), and elsewhere.

35 J.S. Mill, "Lord Durham and the Canadians," *London and Westminster Review* 28 (1838): 522.

36 Roebuck proposes an elective upper house for the colonies when he is speaking as the representative of the Assembly of Lower Canada. When he is speaking for himself, he recommends abolition (see, for example, Hansard, 3, 36 [March 6, 1837], 1335–54). In the constitution he sketched in his memorandum for Durham, he makes no provision for an upper chamber.

37 Several articles by Chapman in the *Canadian Portfolio* list the names and salaries of the council members in each province, in order to demonstrate the narrowness of the circle of friends and relatives holding office and the character of the rewards they obtained for themselves.

38 Compare, *Report* 150–1, 279–80; Craig edition, 81, 140.

39 *Report,* 81–100; Craig edition, 57–61. Roebuck, as agent for the assembly, was one of these officers.

40 *Report,* 81; Craig edition, 58.

41 *Report,* 101; Craig edition, 62.

42 *Report,* 148, and elsewhere; Craig edition, 80.

43 *Report,* 78; Craig edition, 56.

44   *Report,* 278; Craig edition, 139.
45   *Report,* 256, 287, 328; Craig edition, 145, 170.
46   *Report,* 278, 279; Craig edition, 139.
47   Craig, "Introduction," in Craig (ed.), *Lord Durham's Report: An Abridgement of Report on the Affairs of British North America by Lord Durham* (Toronto: McClelland and Stewart, Carleton Library 1968), vi.
48   Ormsby, *The Emergence of the Federal Concept,* 4.
49   See, for example, H.T. Dickinson, *Liberty and Property: Political Ideology in Eighteenth-Century Britain* (London: Weidenfield and Nicolson 1977); A.H. Birch, *Representative and Responsible Government* (Toronto: University of Toronto Press 1964).
50   See John Stewart, "Strengthening the Commons," *Journal of Canadian Studies* 14 (1979): 35–7.
51   *Report,* 79; Craig edition, 56. It has often been argued that "responsible government" was not well established in Britain until shortly before Durham described it in the Report. Phillip A. Buckner (*The Transition to Responsible Government: British Policy in British North America, 1815–1850* [Westport, CT: Greenwood Press 1985]) notes that Aileen Dunham was the first Canadian historian to put forward this view. The most recent writer to make much of it is probably J.M. Ward (*Colonial Self-Government: The British Experience, 1759–1856* [London: Macmillan 1976]). Buckner himself argues that "although some of the constitutional conventions of the eighteenth century were to be displaced by others in the nineteenth century ... the essential principle that the ministers of the Crown were responsible to Parliament for the general conduct of the executive government was clearly established with the eighteenth century" (*The Transition to Responsible Government,* 5).
52   *Report,* 76; Craig edition, 54.
53   *Report,* 74–7; Craig edition, 53–5.
54   *Report,* 280; Craig edition, 141.
55   *Report,* 277; Craig edition, 139.
56   *Report,* 286; Craig edition, 144. Durham further proposed an "adequate" civil list, that is, a list of those executive officers and judges who were to be guaranteed salaries without a vote in the assembly. The Assembly of Lower Canada had fought against the civil list for years (*Report,* 75–6, 327; Craig edition, 53, 54, 170). Another measure, intended to have the effect of strengthening the executive while still recognizing the "inherent" powers of the assembly, was the proposal to divide the work of the executive council into departments. It had been colonial practice to allow each member of the executive to take part in all business brought before it (*Report,* 110; Craig edition, 65, 66). A cabinet of ministers, each responsible for the work of a department, would be a very much stronger and more efficient group, but this concentration of executive power would also provide the popular body with that clear view of executive programs that would enable critical assessment.

57   *Report,* 90, and see, 148, 153; Craig edition, 80, 83.

58   *Report,* 152; Craig edition, 82.

59   Ibid., *Report* and Craig edition.

60   *Report,* 155; Craig edition, 84.

61   *Report,* 33; Craig edition, 30.

62   *Report,* 58–62; Craig edition, 43–5.

63   *Report,* 83; Craig edition, 59.

64   Buller, *Responsible Government for the Colonies,* in E.M. Wrong, *Charles Buller and Responsible Government* (Oxford: Clarendon Press 1929), 92, 93.

65   Edward Gibbon Wakefield, "Sir Charles Metcalfe in Canada," in Wrong, *Charles Buller and Responsible Government,* 185.

66   Ibid, 188.

67   Buller, *Responsible Government,* 84.

68   Wakefield, "Sir Charles Metcalfe," 171.

69   For my understanding of the eighteenth-century mixed-government theorists, I am indebted to H.T. Dickinson for his book of selections from writings by Jonathan Swift, Lord Robert Molesworth, Joseph Addison, John Trenchard and Thomas Gordon, Bolingbroke, David Hume, Edward Spelman, Robert Wallace, John Wilkes, Joseph Priestley, and others (Dickinson [ed.], *Politics and Literature in the Eighteenth Century* [London: Dent 1974]). I have also drawn on his *Liberty and Property: Political Ideology in Eighteenth-Century Britain* (London: Weidenfeld and Nicolson 1977). A book that I did not see until after this chapter had been written is M.J.C. Vile, *Constitutionalism and the Separation of Powers* (Oxford: Clarendon Press 1967). Vile supports many of my contentions. He argues, for example, that essential features of the eighteenth-century constitution, such as the separation of powers, can still be seen in some aspects of today's parliamentary systems, and maintains (here he certainly differs from Dickinson) that the mixed or balanced constitution secured the freedom of the populace in general, and not merely the advantage of the upper class.

70   Hansard, 2, 5 (April 17, 1821), 365.

71   Gareth Jones (ed.), *The Sovereignty of the Law: Selections from Blackstone's Commentaries on the Laws of England* (Toronto: University of Toronto Press 1973), 65–71.

72   See for example Hansard 2, 5 (April 17, 1821), 366, where he refers to the annual parliaments of the reign of Edward II, and notes that the Triennial Act was passed in the time of William and Mary and the Septennial Act by George I. Later, arguing in a general fashion for the extension of the franchise, he says: "Our minds, it seems, are still to be alarmed by visions of anarchy and confusion, to be realized whenever people are put in possession of those elective privileges which our ancestors once peaceably enjoyed."

73   That is, Durham cannot claim that the ballot had once been British practice, like annual parliaments or a broader franchise. But as H.T. Dickinson notes, it had been among the reforms urged by eighteenth-century country gentlemen.

74 *Speeches of the Earl of Durham in Scotland,* 18–19. The eminent whigs of his father's generation and before – Charles James Fox in particular – were always his heroes. Throughout his career he describes himself as heir to their tradition. This was the theme of his speeches at the Fox anniversary dinners in 1819 and 1821, for example. For these speeches, see John Reid (ed.), *Sketch of the Political Career of the Earl of Durham* (Glasgow: John Reid and Co. 1835), 71–3, 97, 98. Durham often refers to motions for parliamentary reform initiated by Fox, by Charles Grey, and by William Lambton, (his father), and above all to the program set forth in the petition laid before Parliament in 1793 by the association known as The Friends of the People, of which William Lambton and Charles Grey were leading members (*Hansard's Parliamentary History, 1066–1803,* 30; 787–99).

75 From a letter to Russell Bowlby, July 8, 1837, which was intented for circulation and publication. For the letter, see New, *Lord Durham,* 314.

76 Hansard, 2, 5 (April 17, 1821), 364, 365.

77 Ibid., 383.

78 Ibid., 3, 3 (March 28, 1831), 1028–9.

79 *Report,* 280; Craig edition, 141.

80 See, for example, *Report,* 34, 35, 37; Craig edition, 30, 31, 33. Some historians argue that although the Radicals speak of the "people," they should be understood as having only middle-class interests in mind. The same charge can be levelled against the whigs (see D.J. Rowe, "Class and Political Radicalism in London, 1831–32," *The Historical Journal* 13 [1970]). I suggest that the charge is no more true of the whigs than of the Radicals, and that, in fact, the whig doctrine allows a livelier sense of the probable opposition between those of "middle rank" and the "lower classes." Durham does not think of middle-class spokesmen as necessarily articulating a coherent interest they share with the lower class, or, indeed, as necessarily expressing their own class interest at the expense of the lower. It is true that he believes that the middle classes will provide the leaders. This means that there will be spokesmen of the "middle rank" for the many interests of the working classes as well as for those of the middle classes. And this is not a bad picture of politics in his time – or later. Many of the reforms he proposed in Britain were intended to bring the new middle-class leaders of popular interests into government, and much of his political support came from such men. See his praise for those of "middle-rank" in Hansard, 2, 5 (April 17, 1821), and 3, 12 (May 22, 1832), and his speech at Newcastle in November 1834 (John Reid, *Sketch,* 383).

81 *Report,* 312; Craig edition, 162.

82 *Report,* 303; Craig edition, 156.

83 *Report,* 268, 269; Craig edition, 133.

84 *Report,* 311, 312; Craig edition, 161, 162.

85 Zera Fink, in *The Classical Republicans: An Essay in the Recovery of a Pattern of Thought in Seventeenth-Century England* (Evanston, IL: Northwestern

University Press 1962), has traced the introduction of the idea of mixed government into British political thought. See also Leo Strauss's review of *The Classical Republicans* in *What is Political Philosophy? And Other Studies* (Glencoe, IL: Free Press 1959) 290–2. Strauss points to differences between the ancient doctrine of mixed government and the modern, implicit in Fink's account.

86   The most contentious debates of this period with respect to creation of new peers had to do with the passage of the Reform Bill through the Lords. Durham was one of those who argued for creation of peers at that time.

87   Stuart Reid, *Life and letters of the First Earl of Durham, 1792–1840*, vol. 2 (London: Longman's Green 1906), 116.

88   Reid, *Life and Letters*, 115.

89   *Report*, 130–1; Craig edition, 69, 70.

90   *Report*, 287, 90. And see 48; Craig edition, 145, 37.

91   See chapter seven.

92   *Report*, 158; Craig edition, 82.

93   Bentham, "Plan of Parliamentary Reform," 527–8.

94   *Report*, 33, 58; Craig edition, 30, 43. For reasons we can well imagine – surely because he expected Papineau to return to take a leading role in Canadian politics in future years – he is careful not to associate Papineau's name with such terms.

95   *Report*, 17; Craig edition, 23.

96   See Ajzenstat, "Modern Mixed Government: A Liberal Defence of Inequality," *Canadian Journal of Political Science* 18 (March 1985).

97   In "Modern Mixed Government" I trace the background from Machiavelli's arguments in the *Discourses*. I must acknowledge the influence of Harvey C. Mansfield, Jr. He guided me through the *Discourses* in *Machiavelli's New Modes and Orders: A Study of the Discourses on Livy* (Ithaca: Cornell University Press 1979) and prompted thoughts about the mixed regime in the twentieth century through his *The Spirit of Liberalism* (Cambridge, MA: Harvard University Press 1978).

98   *Report*, 325, 326; Craig edition, 168, 169.

99   See, for example, Lord Gosford's General Report of 1836. "Although the system of checks and balances is often considered the peculiar feature of the British Constitution, we hope that there are not at present any elements of discord in it of the nature of those which unfortunately exist between the two branches of the Canadian Legislature. The British Government is not, on the one hand, a mere machine sustained by one power, and owing its regularity to the due subordination of all its parts; neither is it, on the other, a system of antagonist forces, keeping each other in order by their mutual repulsion. It is a system, we would rather say, of bodies, which, though, in their origin they acted repulsively on each other, have been brought into harmony by a conviction of slow growth, that to combine is better than to compete" (*British Sessional Papers*, House of Commons, vol. 24, 6, 1837).

100 Tocqueville, *De la Démocratie en Amérique*, tome 1 (Paris: Garnier-Flammarion 1981), 351; and see 344, 365, 359, and 360, where he quotes from *The Federalist*, no. 51.

101 Tocqueville, *De la Démocratie*, 1: 349.

CHAPTER SEVEN

1 *Report*, 14, 15; Craig edition, 20, 21.

2 *Report*, 21; Craig edition, 25.

3 *Report*, 15; Craig edition, 21.

4 *Report*, 27.

5 *Report*, 16; Craig edition, 22, 23.

6 See William Ormsby, *The Emergence of the Federal Concept in Canada* (Toronto: University of Toronto Press 1969), chapter one. Lucas comments, "How then can there ever have been any doubts whatever that the troubles in Lower Canada were mainly due to race" (C.P. Lucas [ed.], *Lord Durham's Report on the Affairs of British North America* [Oxford: Clarendon Press 1912, 3 vols], 3: 127, 128).

7 Lucas, *Lord Durham's Report*, 3: 340.

8 See, for example, Chester New, *Lord Durham: A Biography of John George Lambton, First Earl of Durham* (Oxford: Clarendon Press 1929), 489.

9 One missive from the merchants reads: "The evils engendered by the distinctiveness of national origin, and the prejudices of opposite and antagonistic races ... will remain to wither ... remedial measures unless they shall be accompanied by the Union of the Canadas" (cited in Ormsby, *The Emergence of the Federal Concept in Canada*, 19.

10 Hansard, Series 3, 36 (March 6, 1837).

11 "It has been my ruling principle throughout my political life to endeavour to bring all classes ... within the pale of the true, not the spurious constitution" (from the letter to Russell Bowlby, cited in New, *Lord Durham*, 315). "I have never yet, nor ever will, conceal my sentiments, whether addressing Radicals on the one hand, or Tories on the other. I have over and over avowed what my principles are. I hold that in our form of government by King, Lords and Commons, there will be found as great a degree of liberty ..." (*Speeches of the Earl of Durham Delivered at Public Meetings in Scotland in 1834* [London: James Ridgway and Sons 1838], 18, 19). The speeches in this volume especially strike this note.

12 British and colonial thinkers alike seemed to have thought of the colonies at this time as a political tabula rasa on which they could write according to belief and doctrine. The various unions, the American-style electoral institutions – the possibilities seemed vast, suggesting that it was the 1830s and 1840s that should be regarded as the period of Canada's founding.

13 See *Report*, 65–8; Craig edition, 47–9. Durham cites passages from the Proclamation of 1763, and from the Commission of Governor-in-Chief James Murray, offering grants of land in Quebec to British soldiers and settlers from other

provinces for the purpose of encouraging British immigration into French-speaking areas. He compares this with instructions from England in 1775 directing that grants of land, even to British immigrants, be made in fief and seigneury. His point is one noted before: the British government had failed to follow either of the "two modes by which a government may deal with a conquered territory" (see chapter one). Had the policy of encouraging the French nationality been followed, the populations should have been allocated widely separate areas of the country. Had the policy of assimilation been followed, no change of law was more necessary than that facilitating the alienation of land. Durham refers to the Quebec Act on 116, 117, and to the Constitutional Act of 1791 on 138, 220 of the *Report*; see the Craig edition, 69, 73, 116.

14   For Roebuck's views on the legislative council, see Hansard 3, 33 (May 16, 1836) and 3, 36 (March 6, 1837). Compare *Report*, 150, 151; Craig edition, 80. For Roebuck on the executive council, see above, chapter six.

15   See chapter six and note 22 below.

16   *Report*, 17, 18, 19; Craig edition, 23, 24.

17   Roebuck's preference for the independence of Lower Canada can be seen in his correspondence with Papineau. He supported the French-Canadian cause in the Rebellion of 1837 and argued for the federation of all the British North American colonies in the scheme for the government of the colonies that he drew up for Durham in 1838 (see *The Colonies of England: A Plan for the Government of Some Portion of Our Colonial Possessions* [London: John W. Parker 1849], 193–220). See also Hansard 3, 37 (April 14, 1837).

18   See *Report*, 304, 305; Craig edition, 157, 158.

19   Roebuck, "Affairs of Canada," *The Westminster Review* 46 (October, 1835): 146.

20   Roebuck, *Existing Difficulties in the Government of the Canadas* (London: C. and W. Reynell 1836), 25.

21   The French Canadians, he said on one occasion, were "endowed with the same spirit of liberality which prevailed throughout the continent on which they lived" (Hansard 3, 33 [May 16, 1836]).

22   Roebuck, *Existing Difficulties*, 26.

23   "I solemnly charge the Executive for the last twenty years with disgracefully and most corruptly endeavouring to create and perpetuate national and religious hatred among a large body of his Majesty's subjects, and, for their private and paltry purposes, of stirring up and maintaining amongst those who ought to be brethren something nearly approximating the direful calamities of a civil war" (Hansard 3, 22 [April 15, 1834]). And see Roebuck, *Colonies of England*, 201; *Existing Difficulties*, 26, 27, 28; and "Affairs of Canada," 151.

24   *Report*, 16, 17; Craig edition, 23.

25   *Report*, 16, 17, 62, 63, 72, 73; Craig edition, 23, 46, 52.

26   *Report*, 57; Craig edition, 42.

27   *Report*, 134, 135.

28   Ibid., 24.

29   For discussion of virtue, freedom, and civilization, see chapter three.

30   *Report*, 27; Craig edition, 26.

31   *Report*, 289, 27; Craig edition, 146, 26.

32   *Report*, 63; Craig edition, 46.

33   *Report*, 303; Craig edition, 156.

34   *Report*, 301; Craig edition, 155.

35   *Report*, 34–36; Craig edition, 30-2.

36   *Report*, 294; Craig edition, 150.

37   See the entire discussion, *Report*, 292–4; Craig edition, 150–1.

38   *Report*, 34, 35; Craig edition, 30, 31.

39   *Report*, 292, 293; Craig edition, 149.

40   *Report*, 22; Craig edition, 25, 26.

41   *Report*, 22, 58; Craig edition, 26, 43.

42   *Report*, 59; Craig edition, 43, 44. As Durham reminds us on this page, he had first elaborated this point in his Dispatch to the Colonial Office of August 9 (see Lucas, *Lord Durham's Report*, 3: 319–31).

43   *Report*, 21; Craig edition, 25.

44   *Report*, 48; Craig edition, 37.

45   *Report*, 23, 36; Craig edition, 32.

46   Compare Alexis de Tocqueville, *De la Démocratie* en Amérique, tome 1 (Garnier-Flammarion 1981), 1: 107–16.

47   *Report*, 24.

48   Ibid., 25, 26.

49   Ibid.

50   Ibid., 135.

51   Ibid., 136; Craig edition, 71.

52   "Report of the Commissioner of Enquiry into the State of Education in Lower Canada," in Lucas, *Lord Durham's Report*, 3: 266.

53   *Report*, 287; Craig edition, 145.

54   *Report*, 31; Craig edition, 28.

55   *Report*, 33, 58; Craig edition, 30.

56   *Report*, 33; Craig edition, 30.

57   These observations may have been confirmed by reports submitted to Durham by his aide, Stewart Derbishire. Derbishire, looking for a "grievance" to explain the Rebellion of 1837, claims to have found none; that is, he found no practical matter of complaint that could be remedied by the home government. He attributed the rebellion to the appeal made by Papineau and his "confederates" to "the nationality of this vain people" (Public Archives of Canada, Durham Papers, MG24, A27, vol. 37. Derbishire's letter to Durham of May 24, 1838.)

58   *Report*, 30; Craig edition, 30.

59   *Report*, 84; Craig edition, 60.

60   *Report*, 37; Craig edition, 32, 33.

61   *Report*, 51; Craig edition, 39.

62 *Report*, 61, 62; Craig edition, 45.
63 *Report*, 17, 72, 58; Craig edition, 23, 52, 44.
64 *Report*, 312; Craig edition, 162.
65 *Report*, 299; Craig edition, 154.
66 See above, note 11.
67 See *Report*, 74; Craig edition, 53, where Durham speaks of the "almost universal" suffrage in the colonies. Even the Radicals did not complain about electoral practices. That was the heart of the problem in Britain in their opinion, but not in British North America.
68 Cynthia Enloe uses the term political "style" in this fashion (*Ethnic Conflict and Political Development* [Boston: Little, Brown 1973]). And see Howard Brotz, "Multiculturalism in Canada: A Muddle," *Canadian Public Policy* 6 (1980).
69 Marvin Zetterbaum, *Tocqueville and the Problem of Democracy* (Stanford: Stanford University Press 1967), 85.
70 Tocqueville, *De la Démocratie*, 1: 257.
71 Ibid., 257, 258. "L'Amérique a eu de grands partis; aujourd'hui ils n'existent plus; elle y a beaucoup gagné en bonheur, mais non en moralité."
72 *Report*, 289; Craig edition, 146.
73 *Report*, 30, 31, 29; Craig edition, 28, 29, 27.
74 *Report*, 294, 295; Craig edition, 150, 151.
75 *Report*, 299; Craig edition, 154.
76 *Report*, 293; Craig edition, 149.

CHAPTER EIGHT

1 David Cameron, *Nationalism, Self-Determination and the Quebec Question* (Toronto: Macmillan 1974), 2.
2 McRoberts and Posgate, *Quebec, Social Change and Political Crisis* (Toronto: McClelland and Stewart 1980), chapters 1 and 6.
3 Kenneth McRae, "The Plural Society and the Western Political Tradition," *Canadian Journal of Political Science* 12 (1970), 682, 688.
4 Vernon Van Dyke, "Collective Entities and Moral Rights: Problems in Liberal Democratic Thought," *The Journal of Politics* 44 (1982): 21; "The Individual, the State and Ethnic Communities in Political Theory," *World Politics* 29 (1977): 343.
5 That the change is recent is the point of the article by Means cited in chapter one, "Human Rights and the Rights of Ethnic Groups," *International Studies Notes* 1 (1974). See also the very similar argument by Nathan Glazer and Daniel Moynihan, "Why Ethnicity," *Commentary* 58 (1974). They remark that social scientists have been "surprised by the persistence and salience of ethnic-based forms of identification." It has not been generally recognized, they argue, that ethnicity is a "new social category as significant for the understanding of the present-day world as that of social class itself."

6   See Howard Brotz, "Comments," *Canadian Public Policy* 8 (1982): 613: "My ... criticism of the multiculturalism policy in Canada is that it was one small step towards the politicization of ethnicity. By this I mean bringing into being a political situation in which the rights, privileges and disabilities of individuals are *legally* defined on the basis of their ethnic group membership. Apartheid in South Africa is a very good example."

7   Charles Taylor, "Why Do Nations Have to Become States" in Stanley French (ed.), *Philosophers Look at Confederation* (Montreal: Canadian Philosophical Association 1979), 25. For an argument that it is the very loss of absolutes, especially religious absolutes, that has led men to invest history, origin, and nationality, with such importance in the modern world, see Anthony D. Smith, *The Ethnic Revival* (Cambridge: Cambridge University Press 1981).

8   Cameron, *Nationalism, Self-Determination and the Quebec Question*, 8; Taylor, "Why Do Nations Have to Become States."

9   Marcel Rioux, *Quebec in Question* (Toronto: Lorimer 1971). And see his article, "The Development of Ideologies in Quebec," in Orest M. Kruhlak, Richard Schultz, and Sidney I. Pobihushchy (eds), *The Canadian Political Process: A Reader*, revised edition (Toronto: Holt, Rinehart and Winston 1973).

10 See Rioux, *Quebec in Question*, 100. Georges Grant writes: "In Mr. Trudeau's writings, there is evident distaste for what was by tradition his own, and what is put up along with that distaste are universalist goods which will be capable of dissolving that tradition" ("Nationalism and Rationality," in Abraham Rotstein (ed.), *Power Corrupted: The October Crisis and the Repression of Quebec* (Toronto: New Press 1971), 52. See also Denis Smith, *Bleeding Hearts ... Bleeding Country* (Edmonton: M.G. Hurtig 1971), 132, and the whole of chapter 6.

11 Rioux, *Quebec in Question*, 72.

12 William Ormsby, "Lord Durham and the Assimilation of French Canada," in Norman Penlington (ed.), *On Canada: Essays in Honour of Frank Underhill* (Toronto: University of Toronto Press 1969), 52, 53. James de Wilde, "The Parti Québécois in Power," in Richard Simeon (ed.), *Must Canada Fail?* (Montreal: McGill-Queen's University Press 1977), 20.

13 Rioux, *Quebec in Question*, 113.

14 Claude Morin, *Quebec versus Ottawa: The Struggle for Self-Government 1960–72* (Toronto: University of Toronto Press 1976), 155, 156.

15 Peter Burroughs, *The Canadian Crisis and British Colonial Policy* (Toronto: Macmillan 1972), 5.

16 Rioux, *Quebec in Question, 4*.

17 Ibid., 127, and see translator's note, footnote 3.

18 Léon Dion, "Towards a Self-Determined Consciousness," in Dale C. Thomson (ed.), *Quebec Society and Politics* (Toronto: McClelland and Stewart 1975), 26–38.

19 McRoberts and Posgate, *Quebec, Social Change and Political Crisis*, chapter 6 especially. For a critique of the new middle-class thesis, see William D. Coleman, *The Independence Movement in Quebec, 1945–1980* (Toronto: University

of Toronto Press 1984), 5–13. Coleman argues that there was no such identifiable class before the Quiet Revolution, and that the changes of the early 1960s were brought in by alliance of francophone businessmen, organized labour, and the traditional middle class.

20   McRoberts and Posgate, *Quebec, Social Change and Political Crisis*, 104.

21   See Taylor, *The Pattern of Politics* (Toronto: McClelland and Stewart 1970), chapter 5.

22   Taylor, "Why Do Nations Have to Become States?" 26, 27.

23   For consociational democracy in the Canadian and European contexts, see McRae (ed.), *Consociational Democracy: Political Accommodation in Segmented Societies (Toronto: McClelland and Stewart 1963)*, esp. McRae's own contributions.

24   McRae, "Consociationalism and the Canadian Political System," in *Consociational Democracy*, 252.

25   McRae, "Introduction," in his *Consociational Democracy*, 8.

26   It was not my intention to do more than dip into the ocean of material on nationalism. I should mention that a much fuller account of nationalism as a function of economic factors and ambition than can be discussed here can be found in Ernest Gellner's work: see his *Nations and Nationalism* (Oxford: Basil Blackwell 1983). I am grateful to Ramsay Cook for bringing several books to my attention, among them the books I have noted by Gellner and Anthony Smith.

27   McRae, "The Plural Society and The Western Political Tradition"; and Van Dyke, "Collective Entities" and "The Individual, The State and Ethnic Communities."

28   Reginald Whitaker, "The Quebec Cauldron," in Michael S. Whittington and Glen Williams (eds), *Canadian Politics in the 1980s*, 2nd ed. (Toronto: Methuen 1984), 35. "I am inclined to think," argues John D. Jackson, "that it is not possible to have a pluralism of national identity while at the same time maintaining an equality of opportunity" (*Community and Conflict: A Study of French-English Relations in Ontario* [Toronto: Holt, Rinehart and Winston 1975], 156). "In sum, from the classical liberal perspective, the nationalist demand for self-determination, though often clothed in democratic rhetoric, appears rather as a form of the traditional inegalitarian claim to rule on behalf of a particular way of life" (Rainer Knopff, "Liberal Democracy and the Challenge of Nationalism in Canadian Politics," *Canadian Review of Studies in Nationalism* 9 [1982]).

29   This would cast Pierre Trudeau's arguments in a much kinder light than was suggested in note 10. See Trudeau, "Quebec and the Constitutional Problem," in Trudeau, *Federalism and the French Canadians* (Toronto: Macmillan 1968), 15. He argues that the middle class has more to gain "from a separate Quebec, for, in fact, this group will provide the new ruling class."

30   McRae, "Introduction," *Consociational Democracy*, 7.

31   See Cynthia Enloe, *Ethnic Conflict and Political Development* (Boston: Little, Brown 1973), for an argument that leads to the conclusion that programs of multiculturalism promote assimilation. Denis Smith remarks on a study that appears

to indicate that the provision of advanced educational opportunities in French actually speeds, rather than slows, assimilation (F.G. Vallée and N. Shulman, "The Viability of French Groupings outside Quebec," in Mason Wade [ed.], *Regionalism in the Canadian Community, 1867–1967* [Toronto: University of Toronto Press 1969], cited in Smith's *Bleeding Hearts*, 125). But for the most comprehensive account of the way in which programs and policies designed to advanced economic development, and more important, policies meant to preserve culture and language, can speed assmilation, see Coleman, *The Independence Movement in Quebec*, esp. chapter 7, "Language Policy and Cultural Development."

Index